SOUTHWEST
FRUIT & VEGETABLE GARDENING

*Plant, Grow, and Harvest
the Best Edibles*

© 2014 Quarto Publishing Group USA Inc.

First published in 2014 by Cool Springs Press, an imprint of The Quarto Group, 401 Second Avenue North, Suite 310, Minneapolis, MN 55401, USA. T (612) 344-8100 F (612) 344-8692 www.QuartoKnows.com

Cool Springs Press titles are also available at discount for retail, wholesale, promotional, and bulk purchase. For details, contact the Special Sales Manager by email at specialsales@quarto.com or by mail at The Quarto Group, Attn: Special Sales Manager, 401 Second Avenue North, Suite 310, Minneapolis, MN 55401, USA.

ISBN-13: 978-1-59186-614-5

Library of Congress Cataloging-in-Publication Data

Soule, Jacqueline A.
  Southwest fruit & vegetable gardening : plant, grow, and harvest the best edibles / Jacqueline A. Soule.
    pages cm
  Other title: Southwest fruit and vegetable gardening
  Includes index.
  ISBN 978-1-59186-614-5 (sc)
  1. Gardening--Southwestern States. 2. Fruit--Southwestern States. 3. Vegetables--Southwestern States. 4. Herbs--Southwestern States. I. Title. II. Title: Southwest fruit and vegetable gardening.
  SB453.2.S68S68 2014
  635.0979--dc23
                        2014012723

Acquisitions Editor: Mark Johanson
Design Manager: Cindy Samargia Laun
Layout: S. E. Anglin

Printed in USA

SOUTHWEST
FRUIT & VEGETABLE GARDENING

*Plant, Grow, and Harvest
the Best Edibles*

JACQUELINE A. SOULE

**COOL
SPRINGS
PRESS**

CONTENTS

PREFACE

Growing up gardening here in the Southwest, I did not always know the why of planting different crops in different seasons, it was just how it was done. Now that I have the Ph.D. I know the science as well, and it is all in the genes. Luckily, you don't need to get a degree, this book sorts it out for you and helps you plant the right crop in the right season.

Organization of this Book

The science of gardening reveals that some plants have tropical ancestors and heat-loving genes, and thus flourish in the warm season. Other plants have genes that help them thrive in cool soils and cooler seasons. Thus, if you want to successfully garden in the Southwest, you need to encourage plants to fulfill their genetic destiny, be it warm or cool.

This is a warm and cool book. And really, isn't that how we garden and approach life too? "Oh gee, it's April already, what should I be doing right now?" If it's life, you might be thinking taxes, but if it is in the garden, it depends where you live in the Southwest. In April in the Cold Mountains

Once you've tried a home-grown carrot, you'll never want to go back to store-bought.

some folks have just made their last ski run and are looking to start some nice cool-season crops like greens and root crops. In April in the Low Desert, temperatures are heading toward triple digits and it is time to plant the warm-season crops like melons and corn. Don't be grumpy that this is not an A to Z book. As friend Katie Elzer-Peters says, "Gardens are not alphabetized." (That is what the indices and plant lists are for.)

Two Pieces of Advice

Give yourself permission to get it wrong.

Some of my first memories are of "helping" in the gardens of my grandparents from both sides. My first scientific experiment was encouraged by my father who taught me about control groups ("Let's put cow patties on only half of the plants, honey") and I have been learning about gardening ever since. A garden buddy who is now 92 years old claims that he too learns new things from his garden each year. This is to encourage you. Gardening is both an art and a science, and Mother Nature keeps changing the playing field with variables such as late frosts and fierce windstorms. I have learned that plants die, and you may never know why, but you need to just keep on experimenting and trying. Did you forget to get your onions in in January in the Middle Desert? Experiment. Try planting them in February. You may have less of a crop, but you should get something.

Gardening is part of nature, not a sterile environment.

You are going to get dirty and your food is going to have dirt on it and have some damage from garden pests. A few holes in the leaves or spots on the fruit do not render food inedible and does not mean you need to get out the toxic chemicals and spray for pests. Your garden (especially in our arid environment) will not look like those lovely photo-shopped magazine covers. Real life is not a Hollywood runway, or a supermarket produce aisle. There are many actors that don't make the red carpet and tons and tons of produce that is fed to livestock. When it comes to food you grow, if it tastes good and is healthy for you and your family, a few blemishes do not matter.

My all-time hero is Ms. Frizzle, from the *Magic Schoolbus*. In her immortal words, "Get messy, take chances, make mistakes!" I think Ms. Frizzle had to be a gardener in her off-duty hours. Now go forth and garden!

—Jacqueline

DEDICATION

For Paul

ACKNOWLEDGMENTS

Over the years, so many people have encouraged me, my love for plants and the outdoors, my delight in creatively crafting prose, not to mention my dedication to scientific accuracy. There are too many people to name (including some whose names I never learned). I expect that until the day I die I will be giving forward the kindnesses I have received over the years. That said, here are a few folks who stand out and deserve thanks for their assistance in helping me become the gardener and garden writer I am today: Merle Allen Soule, Henry Mandelbaum, Roz Spicer, Cynthia Baker, Ramsey Sealy, Shirley Owens, Dean Rucker, Barbara Dore, Tim Clark, Paul Meyer, Billie Lee Turner, Harold Robinson, Matt Johnson, present and former members of the Arizona Native Plant Society, Scott Millard, Eric A. Johnson, Gilbert White, Mary Fish, Mark Evans, and the many other editors through the years.

I especially want to thank all of the present and former members of the Garden Writers Association, starting with the judges in 1986 who thought my writing was worthy of an award and started this whole ball rolling. Thanks go out to all the GWA folk who helped with advice, clarification, and tidbits of knowledge from their corners of the various USDA zones.

Kinja and Shira did their share of helping, but this book would not be possible without the love, support, and endless patience of my darling, Paul.

PART I

GROWING EDIBLES IN THE SOUTHWEST

Your chances of success as a gardener will be far greater if you remember one key fact. Plants are living, breathing organisms—just like humans. Just like humans, plants need food, water, shelter, and air to breathe.

Red and yellow chili peppers

Pomegranates require both the heat of the summer and a few weeks of chilling hours in winter.

This book covers the topics you need to be a successful gardener in the Southwest.

Gardening within the Southwest—regional differences in soil, climate
patterns, rainfall, average temperatures, and so on.

Seasonal gardening—there are five gardening seasons in some areas, and
how you can make the most of the two main growing seasons.

Garden planning—get the most out of your space, be it large or small.

Soil—critical, and one of the most challenging aspects to gardening in
the Southwest.

Selecting plants—varieties best for our area, whether to buy seeds or
seedlings, and how to plant them.

Maintaining the garden—watering techniques, when to fertilize, how to
mulch, dealing with pests, and so forth.

USDA PLANT HARDINESS ZONE MAPS

Arizona, Nevada, and New Mexico

The United States Department of Agriculture (USDA) produces a Plant Hardiness Zone Map that indicates the average minimum cold temperatures, in the United States, which serves a handy purpose but is not all you need to know when it comes to growing plants in the Southwest.

With wide geographic variation in the Southwest comes vast climate variation. The USDA Zone map, based on days of freezing temperatures in a year, offers us fourteen USDA zones in our three states, from Zone 4a to Zone 10b. These zones do not tell the whole story, because we also have searing summer temperatures, single-digit humidity, not to mention constant drying wind and vast mountain ranges that thrust into the sky, changing the weather up and down their slopes. Even within a single city, the zones can vary three notches. In winter are you down along the cold river or up on a south-facing mountain slope? What does the wind do in your yard?

So why print the maps? The USDA maps help you when it comes to selecting fruit trees, and when to plant in each of the five seasonal gardens. But be warned—USDA maps are based on the amount of cold not heat or aridity, and not every plant you see rated for your specific zone will survive in our harsh climate.

ZONE	Average Minimum Temperature		ZONE		
4A	-25 to -30		7B	10 to 5	
4B	-20 to -25		8A	15 to 10	
5A	-15 to -20		8B	20 to 15	
5B	-10 to -15		9A	25 to 20	
6A	-5 to -10		9B	30 to 25	
6B	0 to -5		10A	35 to 30	
7A	5 to 0		10B	40 to 35	

Arizona

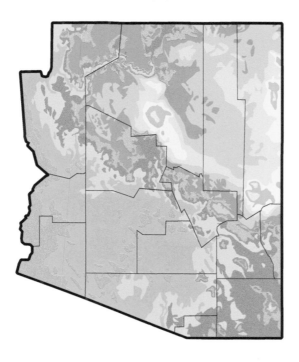

Nevada

New Mexico

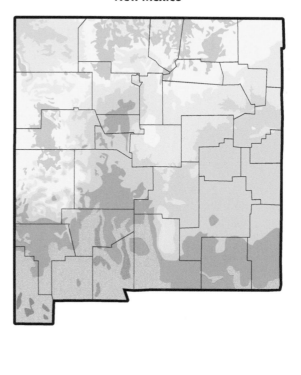

CHAPTER 1

THE SOUTHWEST REGION

Welcome to growing a garden in one of the most fascinating and diverse places on earth. First there is the geographic region itself, with strongly upthrusting mountains, windswept plateaus, and canyons that reach down into the dawn of earth's prehistory. We have elevations close to sea level in Yuma, Arizona, and some of the tallest peaks in the lower forty-eight states, such as the snow-capped San Francisco peaks outside Flagstaff, Arizona, and the Sangre de Cristo Range in New Mexico. Mountains and mesas may be of igneous, metamorphic, or sedimentary rock, providing unique parent material for the soils of our region. (More on soils in Chapter 3, "Building Great Soil.") With this wide geographic variation in the Southwest comes vast climate variation, as much as you could see in a journey from the tip of Florida to the Alaskan tundra.

Gardening Regions in the Southwest

The regions in this book are based on three factors: elevation, USDA hardiness zone, and seasonal rainfall patterns; in other words, your local climate. Even within these five regions, there is huge variation in growing conditions. Indeed, within your own yard, there are variations in growing conditions, termed microclimates. You may be able to grow something not rated for your regional climate by using such highly local microclimates.

Low Desert

Freezes: If freezes occur, between 15 November and 15 February
Summer highs: In the 110°F range
Average summer humidity: 10 to 40 percent
Average winter humidity: 0 to 80 percent
Precipitation: Snow average one winter in fifty, does not stick
   Arizona—Rains winter, annual average 2 to 8 inches, depending on location

Middle Desert

First frost average: 1 November
Last frost average: 15 March
Summer highs: In the 100°F range
Average summer humidity: 10 to 90 percent
Average winter humidity: 0 to 80 percent
Precipitation: Snow average one winter in five, generally does not stick
   Arizona—rains both summer and winter, annual average 6 to 12 inches, depending on location
   Nevada—rains winter, annual average 2 to 6 inches, depending on location
   New Mexico—rains both summer and winter, annual average 6 to 12 inches, depending on location

High Desert

First frost average: 15 October
Last frost average: 15 April
Summer highs: In the upper 90°F range
Average summer humidity: 20 to 70 percent
Average winter humidity: 0 to 30 percent
Precipitation:
   Arizona—rains winter, snow common, annual average 4 to 12 inches, depending on location
   Nevada—rains winter, snow common, annual average 3 to 8 inches, depending on location
   New Mexico—rains summer and winter, snow common, annual average 12 to 20 inches, depending on location

Cool Highlands

First frost average: October 1
Last frost average: May 1
Summer highs: In the lower 90°F range
Average summer humidity: 20 to 45 percent
Average winter humidity: 0 to 30 percent
Precipitation:

> *Arizona*—summer and winter, snow common, annual average 12 to 18 inches
>
> *Nevada*—winter, snow common, annual average 5 to 12 inches, depending on location
>
> *New Mexico*—summer and winter, snow common, annual average 10 to 18 inches

Cold Mountains

First frost average: September 1
Last frost average: June 1
Summer highs: Average in the 80°F range
Average summer humidity: 20 to 45 percent
Average winter humidity: 0 to 30 percent
Precipitation:

> *Arizona*—summer and winter, snow common, annual average 12 to 18 inches
>
> *Nevada*—winter, snow common, annual average 5 to 20 inches, depending on location
>
> *New Mexico*—summer and winter, snow common, annual average 10 to 18 inches

When to Plant

Timing of vegetable planting will be based on where you live and if it is a warm-season or cool-season vegetable. Trees, shrubs, and perennials generally do best planted in early autumn, which gives them a chance to start getting established before winter, or worse, searing summer sun.

Days to Maturity and Frost Tables

Each vegetable has a number of frost-free days that it requires to reach maturity. Radishes can be ready in as few as 30 days, but a melon may need 180 days. If you do not have 180 frost-free days, select a different variety or different crop. The good news is that plant breeders are striving all the time to create plants that mature more quickly. As you use this book, be sure to pay attention to the varieties recommended for your area.

Frost Tables by City

City	Last Probable Spring Freeze	First Probable Fall Freeze	Number of Probable Frost-Free Days
ARIZONA			
Flagstaff	July 7	Sept. 12	60
Nogales	April 27	Oct. 22	196
Page	Nov. 6	March 27	224
Phoenix	Feb. 26	Dec. 16	319
Prescott	June 7	Oct. 5	138
Safford	May 8	Oct. 25	187
Show Low	June 15	Oct. 3	110
Tucson	April 13	Nov. 20	249
Winslow	May 30	Oct. 10	149
Yuma	Feb. 26	Dec. 9	313
NEVADA			
Carson City	June 18	Sept. 9	86
Elko	June 26	Aug. 28	58
Ely	June 22	Sept. 1	71
Las Vegas	April 1	Nov. 18	255
Reno	June 19	Aug. 23	75
Tonopah	May 15	Oct. 15	151
Winnemucca	June 26	Aug. 26	60
NEW MEXICO			
Albuquerque	May 16	Sept. 26	140
Carlsbad	April 24	Oct. 27	199
Clovis	May 13	Oct. 10	162
Gallup	June 30	Sept. 8	76
Lordsburg	May 23	Oct. 18	161
Raton	June 6	Sept. 28	130
Santa Fe	May 20	Sept. 20	128
Taos	June 19	Sept. 20	107
Tucumcari	May 14	Oct. 11	182
Zuni	June 21	Sept. 23	107

CHAPTER 2

SEASONAL GARDENING

Gardening in the Southwest is not like anywhere else on earth, and thus it is tough to find a good gardening book for our distinctive region. We hope we have taken care of that issue here by dividing the plants into two categories: cool-season plants (those that grow best when temperatures are cool—averaging below 70°F) and warm-season plants (those that grow best when temperatures are above 65°F).

For the most part, "warm" and "cool" are descriptors for the temperatures that the plants prefer, but for some there is another key defining factor—day length. Although it is termed "day length" in all the books, plants are actually responding to the number of hours of darkness, not the number of hours of light. Warm-season plants will flower and set fruit as the nights get longer, because their genes are telling them to get their seeds out into the world before the snow flies. Most cool-season plants will flower and set seed when the nights start getting shorter, warning them that the temperatures are about to rise, so they need to get their seeds out in the world before they die of heat prostration.

Success with gardening starts with planting. Putting seeds or plants in the ground at the right time, or starting seeds indoors at the right time for transplanting outdoors, can be vital. Even if the time between planting a cool-season plant like broccoli and a warm-season plant like tomatoes is a bare six weeks, those six weeks can make a big difference.

By and large, you don't need to worry about day length in your vegetable garden—temperature serves as an easy indicator. However, if you find yourself having difficulty with a crop, and you are sure

BIENNIAL VEGETABLES

Annual plants, like most of our vegetables, live their entire life in a single annual cycle—a year. Perennials live for many years. Then there are the odd balls—the biennials. A biennial takes one year to grow, stores its energy for a dormant phase, then uses that energy to flower in the second year. A number of root vegetables have this habit, like parsnips, turnips, and beets. A kissin' cousin to beets is Swiss chard. Also a biennial, this vegetable does well started in a cool garden, often persists in the warm summer garden, and may survive for two years before it bolts and dies.

Swiss chard is a biennial vegetable.

you have everything else correct, search out more information to see if day length is a factor. Your County Cooperative Extension Service maintains a website that provides local information to help you.

Along with the freezing temperatures that are listed in the USDA hardiness zones (remember, "hardy" only refers to the ability to withstand cold) plant growth is also affected by other temperatures—soil temperature, air temperatures, and fluctuations in temperature. In the Southwest, we have to deal with temperatures that soar into the triple digits, often for a triple digit number of days, and all the while single-digit humidity may prevail. Not ideal conditions for any plant. And all these conditions affect when you can plant, when plants flower and set fruit, and harvest times for fruits and vegetables.

But here is the good news: In the Southwest people in the lower elevation regions can usually garden year-round, rotating our crops as the distinctive cool- and warm-growing seasons roll around. At the higher elevations in the Southwest, the seasons compress and your garden will generally include warm- and cool-season crops at the same time.

Garden Seasons of the Southwest

There can be as many as five distinct gardening periods, depending on your region within the Southwest: Autumn, Winter, Spring, Summer, and Monsoon. Gardens in these five seasons may be planted with a blend of warm- and cool-season plants, or may feature only one type.

Low Desert: Plant your cool-season plants from October to March. The rest of the year, select from warm-season plants. The Spring garden will feature plants that like lengthening days, dry beans especially. Summer and Monsoon gardens feature heat lovers like basil and corn. Autumn gardens feature a few cool-season plants like bush beans and the warm-season plants that respond to shortening days, like winter squash.

Middle Desert: Plant your cool-season garden as early as Labor Day, and you can enjoy leafy greens into April. March into May is the Spring garden, and the opportunity to get your tomato fix. Summer gardens start as the temperatures hit 100°F in May with heat-tolerant plants like amaranth. Monsoon gardens are your opportunity to grow myriad native crops, like the Three Sisters—corn, beans, and squash. Autumn gardens feature a few cool-season plants like bush beans and the warm-season plants that respond to shortening days, like winter squash.

High Desert: If you want to plant in containers in a sheltered area, you can have a Winter garden September to April. Otherwise plant your cool-season plants on the shoulders of the warm season, March and April,

The yellow flowers are broccoli plants bolting. The part of the broccoli that we eat is the flower bud. Once the broccoli heads start to bloom, the window of harvest is over.

and September. Warm-season plants can go into the ground after the last frost.

Cool Highlands: If you want to plant in containers in a sheltered area, you can start your Winter garden in February and enjoy to May. Otherwise plant your cool-season plants in the ground in March and April. Warm-season plants can go into the ground after last frost.

Cold Mountains: You can start some cool-season crops in the ground before last frost. Warm-season plants will need to be started indoors and planted in the ground as near to the last frost date as you can.

Bolting

Vegetables and annual herbs that we use the green portion of have two specific growth phases. First is the vegetative stage of growth (yum yum), then comes the flowering stage of growth (all done!). This change to flowering and seed setting is termed "bolting." Most cool-season crops will bolt as the days lengthen and air and soil temperatures rise.

Resist the temptation to let your cool-season plants grow for just a few more days. Cabbages and broccoli are no good once they produce flowers. The exception to this rule are some of the cool-season herbs. Carrot family herbs like cilantro (a.k.a. coriander) and dill produce very useful seeds we use as culinary condiments when they bolt.

Soil Temperature

An inexpensive soil thermometer is an invaluable tool in our area. By checking soil temperature, you can easily see when it is time to plant different edibles. Cool-season vegetable seeds germinate when the soil temperature is at least 50°F. Most of them grow best when soil temperatures are 50°F to 75°F. Warm-season vegetables will not germinate until the soil is above 65°F.

Soil temperatures directly affect disease and pest problems you may experience. Cool, moist soils foster fungi that can attack seeds and rot roots. Warm soils encourage beetle grubs and moth larvae to become active. Plant too soon, your seeds may rot. Plant too late, the grubs may eat your seeds. In the wild, seeds can last for years in the soil, but most vegetable seeds (other than some heirlooms and native crops) have been bred to have human caretakers fussing over them.

Soil thermometer

Air Temperature

New transplants are more affected by air temperature than they are by soil temperature. Cold air, strong winds, or hot dry air can all kill transplants in a heartbeat.

Biological Indicators

One reason why garden books from "Back East" are not helpful in our
area is that they often feature directions with biological indicators
rather than dates or soil temperatures. Instructions to plant a certain
vegetable "when dogwoods are in bloom" are useless in a land with
no dogwoods.

Ask a local old-timer, and he or she may tell you, "Plant tomatoes
when the mesquite leaves are as big as a ground squirrel's ears."
If you are new to the area, this is not very useful information;
besides, if you look at the wrong species of mesquite, you could
be in real trouble.

Ideally, learn your own indicators. Observe what is happening in
and around your yard as you progress through the gardening year,
planting and harvesting your crops. (A garden journal can be a great
assist with this.) Over the years you will learn to sow your last crop
of lettuce as the palo verdes begin to bloom, and harvest your
peaches as the prickly pear fruit ripen.

Fruit-producing plants are also highly affected by air temperatures.
Some plants need a certain number of hours below 45°F in order to produce
fruit (chill hours). Meanwhile some plants head for the compost heap when
the air temperatures drop below 45°F.

Flowers and the fruit they grow into are highly susceptible to air
temperature and humidity. Tomato pollen is not viable at 85°F, and apple or
peach blooms will drop if hit by a late frost—in both of these cases you will
not get the fruit you desire.

Chill Hours

Some like it hot, like citrus, but some do not. Many fruit and nut trees *need*
cooler air to produce their fruit. Termed "chill hours," this is a measure of
the number of hours the air temperature is below 45°F. Plants with chill
hour requirements must meet the minimum number of chill hours in order
to break dormancy and bloom. (Remember—no flowers, no fruits!) A
warm winter may physiologically confuse a fruit tree, causing it to bloom
early, late, or not at all.

Corn plants roll up their leaves to prevent water loss.

WHAT'S WRONG WITH MY CORN?

When corn plants don't have enough water available to take up (the soil is too dry), they will roll their leaves up to reduce the amount of surface area exposed, thus lowering the amount of water lost through the leaves. If the corn leaves are rolled up and "pointy," you need to water the plants!

Heat Exposure

Well, it may be a dry heat, but so is the heat in an oven. Heat affects fruit set just as much as chill requirements, but for a different reason. High air temperatures kill the pollen. Dead pollen can't fertilize the female flowers, and thus you get no fruit. This is especially an issue with crops not native to the Southwest, like tomatoes, cucumbers, and melons.

Temperature Variations Across the Southwest

Elevation, latitude, ambient winds, and proximity to massive mountains all contribute to temperature differences among the regions of the Southwest. The optimal planting time can vary widely between geographically close cities. Prime examples of this are the differences between Las Vegas and Laughlin, Nevada, or Prescott and Phoenix, Arizona, or Albuquerque and Santa Fe, New Mexico. Do your homework with the frost-free charts and specific plant profiles before deciding what to plant and when to plant.

CHAPTER 3

BUILDING GREAT SOIL

My Grandfather used to say, "Dig a ten dollar hole for a two dollar plant." Inflation has set in a tad since Grandpa's days. While the dollar amount may have changed, the concept remains the same. The place where you plant your plants should be lovingly prepared with time, energy, and any soil amendments your plants will need to thrive.

Soil is the place where the roots of the plants become established. Roots absorb water, but at the same time, roots need oxygen so they don't drown. Roots also absorb the minerals a plant requires in order to convert sunlight energy into food. Characteristics of the soil will make it easy or difficult for roots to grow, spread, and absorb the water, minerals, and oxygen a plant needs for life. Time, effort, and money spent in getting the soil to where it needs to be to support healthy plant growth is time and money saved trying to fix problems later.

What You're Starting With: Southwest Soils

Our soils in the Southwest vary widely, even within a single city, or tougher yet, within a single home lot. Soil textures range through clay, coarse sand, gravel, rock, and caliche—we have almost every kind of soil except good loamy fertile garden soil. Clay soils are slow to drain, and dry to rock-like consistency between rains. Sand, gravel, and rocky soils drain very quickly, gravity pulling the water well below the reach of plant roots. And then there is caliche (we will come back to this).

Along with soil texture, soil pH affects plants. Living organisms have a specific pH they do their best at, and plants are no different. Southwest soils are alkaline—they have a high pH value (above

7.0). Most garden plants prefer a slightly acidic environment—a low pH value (below 7.0). Generally our soils range around pH 8.0, while most plants would prefer 6.5 to 7.0 for growing. This is a vast, but not insurmountable, problem.

Add Organic Matter

Books and articles often advocate taking soil samples to a lab for testing before you do anything else. Save your money! No matter what you have (unless it is a long established garden), here in the Southwest you will need to add a great deal of organic matter—compost. If you add this after a soil test, it will change the pH and composition of the soil, rendering your test useless.

When possible, use organic fertilizers that will improve soil health.

Compost is needed in clay soils to help aerate and acidify the soil. Compost is needed in sandy and rocky soils to hold onto water and acidify the soil. Even a long established garden will need compost on an annual basis—because compost is always decaying, plus Southwestern water, from the city or a well, is almost always alkaline, thus pushing the soil back toward an alkaline state.

How to Compost

You can buy compost. It's a quick way to get started. You can also very easily compost at home. However, many home owner associations (HOA) here in the Southwest forbid compost because if the bin or heap is improperly cared for, composting can be troublesome. Hint—you can compost in five-gallon buckets in your garage, with no one the wiser.

Compost Ingredients

There are three components to successfully creating compost in the Southwest: green, brown, and blue. Green ingredients are materials high in nitrogen, like cucumber peels and melon rinds. Brown materials are high in carbon, like shredded newspaper or sawdust. Brown is also a shovel full of soil from your yard. It ought to be rich in the micro-organisms required to do the actual decomposing. Blue represents the water essential to keep everything moist so the micro-organisms can break down the materials into something ready to go into the garden.

Kitchen scraps

Shredded newspaper

Compost with Three Colors

Green

citrus rinds

coffee grounds and tea bags

non-invasive grass clippings*

vegetable kitchen scraps

Brown

shredded paper—junk mail,
    newspaper, paper towels, etc.

sawdust or wood chips

dried leaves—palo verde, pine
    needles, etc.

wheat straw

Blue

keep your compost enclosed and moist

Avoid These!

animal products—meat, dairy, bacon grease, eggshells

weeds gone to seed

Bermudagrass in any form—grass clippings, hay, horse manure

COMPOST TROUBLESHOOTING

Smelly compost is usually too wet. This is easy to fix; just add more brown and dig or turn it in. Shredded paper, sawdust, or straw (never hay), are all easy to add.

If your compost is just sitting there and not shrinking, first try adding some blue. If that doesn't do it, add more green materials plus some more wild soil from your yard to add extra decay micro-organisms.

GO FORTH AND COMPOST

You will need an enclosed space. Open compost heaps and compost piles fail to work in the Southwest. Our air lacks humidity and the materials quickly dry out and cease to decompose.

There are any number of compost bin options on the market, look for fully enclosed ones. If they have air vents, make sure the vents are screened to keep out insect pests. You can build your own bin with cinder blocks, or use 5-gallon buckets with lids, or for an entirely low-tech (and back-breaking) option, dig a hole in the ground and compost in it. Just keep it covered to prevent evaporation.

Add green and brown components as if you were making a giant lasagna. Add ample moisture, and keep the pile "cooking" by turning the compost with a shovel once a week. This helps mix the components and add necessary oxygen. Add more green and brown in equal portions at any time, and blue as needed. One month before you are going to harvest your compost, stop adding any new material.

Important Note: Avoid eggshells because we already have excessive calcium in our soils, and in general we don't need any more. Avoid Bermudagrass in all its forms (grass clippings, hay, horse manure). It will very quickly take over a garden and it takes ages to eradicate it once it starts, even if you use highly toxic compounds.

Soil

Our Southwestern soils have all of the minerals a plant needs for life. But! There is an ogre under the soil.

Plant primary macronutrients are nitrogen (N), phosphorus (P), and potassium (K) and they are the big three traditionally addressed in older gardening tomes. We now know there are secondary macronutrients—calcium (Ca), sulphur (S), magnesium (Mg)—without which plants simply will not thrive. Then there are the micronutrients: boron (B), chlorine (Cl), iron (Fe), manganese (Mn), zinc (Zn), copper (Cu), molybdenum (Mo), and nickel (Ni), all ample in most Southwestern soils. I told you this so you can understand the problem that is *caliche*. We have an abundance of caliche—and it cannot be ignored—because it blocks the uptake of *all* of the essential minerals.

Caliche

Caliche is a form of sedimentary rock, a hardened deposit or layer of calcium carbonate formed a few inches to a few feet beneath the soil.

This calcium carbonate cements together other soil materials, including gravel, sand, clay, and silt. Caliche is generally light colored, from white to light pink to reddish-brown, in layers anywhere from a few inches to a few feet thick, and multiple layers can exist in a single location. Also called hardpan or calcrete, "caliche" is a Spanish word based on the Latin *calx*, meaning lime.

Caliche forms when minerals are leached from the upper layer of the soil and accumulate in layers below the surface, often called caliche "beds." Plants can contribute to the formation of caliche, as well. As the roots take up water, they leave behind the dissolved calcium carbonate, which hardens into caliche. In general, caliche deposition is a slow process, but if enough moisture is present in an otherwise arid site, it can accumulate fast enough to block a drain pipe. Caliche is used in the manufacture of Portland cement, and if the calcium carbonate content is over 80 percent, caliche can be fired and used as a source of lime.

Caliche and Gardening

Caliche causes many problems when trying to grow plants. First, an impermeable caliche layer prevents water from draining properly, which can keep the roots from getting enough oxygen. Also, salts can build up in the soil due to the lack of drainage.

Second, caliche beds prevent plant roots from growing deep into the soil, which means the roots have a limited supply of nutrients, water, and space, and roots can't develop normally. Large trees may not adequately form anchoring roots and can be easily toppled by a heavy wind.

Caliche can be a problem for people wanting to start a garden. Use compost to amend the soil.

Third, caliche beds, even 10 feet down, will still cause the soil to be alkaline. Alkaline soil, along with the calcium carbonate from the caliche, can block plants from taking in nutrients otherwise in the soil, especially iron. An iron deficiency will cause the plant's youngest leaves to become yellow.

What is perhaps most frustrating is that plants do need calcium. Our soil (unless an old sandy river bottom) is rich in the essential nutrients, including calcium, but these are bound by high alkalinity of caliche. Acidifying the soil with compost and other soil additives helps dissolve the caliche and free the essential minerals.

Soil Additives

For caliche-rich alkaline soil, compost is an excellent first step. Compost also fertilizes the soil, but that is discussed under fertilizers (Chapter 5).

Acid

Compost is rich in a natural acid called humeric acid. Peat moss is another excellent and renewable source of soil acid. You can also acidify your soil with used coffee grounds (most coffee shops love to give them away). A treatment of ¼ cup white vinegar in 4 gallons of water is a good way to quickly acidify soil beneath an alkaline-stressed plant. In a large yard or garden, other soil additives can be more effective.

Sulfur

Sulfur is an essential mineral that is used as a soil additive. Sulfur acts to chemically unbind the minerals (nutrients) so that plants can use them. Sulfur is also essential for soil microbes, including the legume symbiotic bacteria. Sulfur is essential for many biological processes in plants and humans, which is one more reason to grow your own food in your own soil.

Sulfur is sold as soil sulfur, sublimed sulfur, flour of sulfur, and "flowers of sulfur." Generally sold in bags, soil sulfur can be added directly to the soil. I prefer to add it into the compost, so microbes have an opportunity to use it and process it into a more usable form for plants.

Note: Too much sulfur can be deadly to any living thing, plants, animals and the soil you are trying to build. Read and follow label instructions. Keep sulfur away from pets, especially self-grooming pets like cats.

Gypsum

Chemically, gypsum is calcium sulfate, and is used commercially to make plaster and wallboard. The calcium that is bound up in caliche is more available to plants in gypsum, plus the sulfate is a form of sulfur that plants and soil microbes can use. If all you are concerned about is a vegetable garden, gypsum can be used according to label instructions. When it comes to trees, gypsum can add to your problems if not used correctly.

Lime

Lime is calcium carbonate, a soil additive used to correct calcium deficiencies and raise pH in acidic soils. Avoid using this product on alkaline soils.

Garden Soil and Topsoil

You could purchase bags of garden soil or topsoil. Unless you lack soil in your yard, it is easier on your wallet to purchase compost and/or peat moss and mix it into your existing soil. My raised beds are a blend of homemade compost, old potting soil, new peat moss, and soil from my yard.

CHAPTER 4

PLANNING & PLANTING YOUR GARDEN

Yes you need to plan before you plant! But everyone has their own way of planning things—some people delight in drawing detailed maps, others like lists, and some like to go with their gut. Any of these approaches will work as long as you consider some key features before you begin planting.

There are seven major points to consider when planning the planting of both vegetables and fruits around your home landscape.

Light tops the critical list when planning your planting. Our low humidity means that there is less moisture in the atmosphere to reduce our intense solar radiation. Southwest sunlight is just plain more intense than other areas of the country. This means that plants from elsewhere may not thrive here.

Sunlight also differs with season. It is not just intensity and duration, but also the angle it slants in at, and thus the microclimate the slanting light produces. A sunny south-facing wall might be good for tender fruit trees in the winter, but such a site may bake them in the summer. The north side of your home may get summer sun, but if sun doesn't strike the soil in winter, it's a poor site for a vegetable garden.

One unique aspect of light to consider in our mostly cloudless Southwest is *reflected light*. It can increase the stress

Planting some annual flowers along with your vegetables will both beautify your garden and attract pollinators.

experienced by a plant. Consider the intensity of sunlight baking in a traditional walled Southwestern yard, then add a swimming pool plus some picture windows and you have an plethora of bouncing light rays far in excess to anything in the natural environment. Many otherwise "full sun" plants bake and die when exposed to these conditions.

Traffic patterns around your home. Vegetable gardens should be sited where they are not "out of sight and out of mind." The closer to the outside door and the kitchen, the better. That said, don't site your garden smack in the way of getting the trash containers to the curb.

Views of blue skies, distant mountains, and our awesome sunsets can sell a home. Bear this in mind as you plan where to place any fruit trees. Alternatively, you may want to plant a grove of trees to hide the neighbor's RV. Be sure to include a check of the views from inside your home as well as out in the yard as you plan your planting.

Water. Hose bibs close to your garden are entirely helpful. Hoses are heavy and running back and forth to turn them on and off gets to be a chore. For fruit trees, some sort of irrigation system would be ideal. Put this in your planning.

Tools left out in the elements is a bad idea. Rust isn't a major problem, but our Southwestern sun will quickly bake wooden handles to a splintery mess and cause fiberglass handles to fray. A little tool shed close to your vegetable garden area is something to consider.

Air flows fairly constantly in the Southwest. It's our mountains, plus the baking days and cool nights. If you have a windy site, vegetables will need to be behind a windbreak. Wind can cause fruit trees to lose their blooms and thus not set fruit. They may need a windbreak as well.

Southwestern wind flows mostly out of the west, but in valleys near mountains the breezes will flow up and down the slopes as well. In winter, cold air falls, and the base of the mountains can be colder than halfway up the slopes. This may affect your choice of fruit trees, and even which winter vegetables you can grow.

Animals. The Southwest abounds with critters, even in densely populated urban centers. Storm drains make wonderful dens and conduits for many species of wildlife. The herbivores that can plague even a city garden include pack rats (AKA roof rats), pocket gophers, antelope ground squirrels, European squirrels, rock squirrels, rabbits, quail, and all manner of fruit-eating birds. In less urban areas add javalinas, skunks, raccoons, coatimundi, ring-tail cats, and deer to the list. These critters make fencing your vegetables and fruit virtually mandatory. Not just because of the furry fiends eating your produce, but because they attract things that eat them, such as rattlesnakes. I share my garden with rattlesnakes, because they eat the pack rats, but I know they are out there and I am intensely wary. Even more so since I almost stepped on a rattler in February.

Since most of our Southwest landscapes come with a walled yard, courtesy of having been colonized by the Spaniards, thus fencing out wildlife is already half accomplished. This is a mixed blessing because it may be harder to find just the right area to site your vegetable garden behind high shady walls. Do make sure your gates and any other openings to your yard are critter-proofed against small rodents and snakes with a dense material such as hardware cloth.

Selecting Plants

There are numerous choices when it comes to deciding what plants to purchase. (Organic? Hybrid? Heirloom?) While I can't decide for you, I can help shed some light on the many options that are out there, and offer what has worked best for me in my many gardens over the decades.

Organic

The term "organic," when used to label a product for sale, means that the product has been produced or grown according to a set of specific standards. Different regulatory agencies have different standards, and the grower must jump through a number of hoops to become certified "organic." In general, the term refers to producing plants without manufactured pesticides. Some states have more stringent labeling rules and require no manufactured chemicals at all, including no manufactured fertilizer, only naturally made compost.

If you want to garden organically, nurturing your soil and the myriad microorganisms that help plants thrive, then start with organic seed, seedlings, or plants. Organically grown products have already proven themselves via "survival of the fittest." You are shelling out money and time and water, so why not get the seed or plant that comes from the most "fit" parent plants?

Plant Pollination and You

Many plants have flowers that invite pollinators to bring in pollen from another plant of the same species, crossing or breeding with distantly related kin. This flow of genes helps plant species survive in an ever-changing environment. Other species are very conservative about who they cross with. As a gardener this means that you can save seed of some vegetables from year to year, but not from others. One example is the squash family. Squash cross readily with other members of the same family, including crosses we may not desire like watermelon and zucchini. While the parents will look and taste just fine, the seeds inside would grow into an inedible waste of time and space.

Hybrids

Humans have been hybridizing plants for millennia. In Mesopotamia, the ancients crossed different dates, until they produced preferred date varieties for sugar quantity and other date varieties for drying ability.

Hybridizing is easy, you take the pollen from one variety of a plant and use it to fertilize another variety, then put a bag over the fertilized flower to keep it from crossing with any others. The seed produced by the fertilized plant are considered *hybrid* seed. Some hybrids must be made each and every time you want a specific variety. Hybrid seed can be produced organically.

Hybrid seed is not the same as GMO (genetically modified organism) seed. The term GMO refers to seed whose genetic

Seed packets will indicate whether the plant is a hybrid or heirloom.

material has been altered using genetic engineering techniques, inserting genes from entirely different life forms into plants. One example of this "novel combination of genetic material obtained through the use of modern biotechnology"* is corn with the bacterium *B.t.* (*Bacillus thuringiensis*) spliced into the seed genes. The bacteria will be found in every cell of the corn plant that grows from that seed. Even small amounts of *B.t.* is deadly to all members of the butterfly family. At this writing, there is preliminary evidence that even moderate amounts of *B.t.* are disruptive to human digestion.

*part of the legal definition of GMO

Open Pollinated and Heirloom

Open pollinated is a term used for a plant that produces stable characteristics from generation to generation when grown in a garden setting. In other words, it often self-pollinates. Arugula is one example of an open-pollinated plant from which you can easily save seed.

The term *heirloom* is used for plant varieties that were popular half a century or more ago, chiefly prior to World War II. Heirloom varieties are generally open-pollinated as well, but the terms are not interchangeable. There are also a number of heirloom fruit trees. If a certain heirloom has historically been grown near you, it should work well in your garden.

Locally Grown versus Out of Town

Ah, the internet. Plants galore to tempt you. Before you head for the computer, know that there are a number of state restrictions shipping plants into our area. Not necessarily a bad thing. This can force you to look for plants that have been grown locally, and have proven themselves to thrive with our highly unique growing conditions. (See *Resources*, page 206.)

Vegetable seed catalogs are a ton of fun to peruse. The folks who write them can make old cardboard sound like the cat's meow. Over the decades, I have discovered that cool-season vegetables can come from any cool-season company, but when it comes to our summers, even in the higher elevations and mountains, you need to turn to Southwestern seed companies to get the varieties that will thrive in our low humidity.

Selecting Healthy Plants

You don't select rotten or bruised fruit at the supermarket, and you shouldn't select damaged merchandise at the nursery either. Resist the urge to buy the mark downs and bargain plants at the end of the season. They are often stressed and diseased. Even if they are healthy, once you factor in your time, not to mention water, fertilizer, etc., plus the risk of bringing pathogens or pest infestation into your yard, the "bargains" seldom are worth it.

Be sure to select healthy plants when buying from your local nursery.

Look for good top growth. Avoid spindly shoots, overly dense growth, sickly foliage, damaged limbs, damaged bark, and plants either too big or too small for their container. Make sure any fruit trees have a single healthy leader. Avoid insect infested or damaged plants. Avoid plants in full bloom—their energy is focused on flowering, not growing new roots.

Look for good root growth. This does not matter so much for annuals, but for shrubs or trees it is important. Ask a nursery worker to show you the sides of the root ball. Avoid plants with diseased or insect-infested roots. Avoid large, ropy, spiraling root systems. Spiral root systems will end up growing in circles and will not send out anchoring roots.

Disease resistance. Many of the plant diseases that are prevalent in other parts of the country are rare in the Southwest. That said, the diseases are hard to get rid of once they get into your soil, so consider planting resistant varieties.

Be considerate. Don't damage other plants reaching through them for the one individual you have your eye on. Yes, plants can heal, but it is hard for them to do so in a nursery setting.

Planting the Vegetable Garden

Some plants are easy to grow from seed, while others are easier if purchased as transplants. This has been noted for each plant profiled in Chapter 7.

Starting Seeds Indoors

If you want to grow varieties that will thrive in our area, you might have to order seeds and grow your own transplants. If you are just starting out, wait until you are more used to caring for plants before you invest in indoor growing. If you wish to try, here are some tips.

Fill tray with seed-sprouting mix, and plant seeds according to package instructions.

Cover seeds until they sprout.

Necessary Supplies
Seed-starting mix
Seedling trays
Clear plastic covers

Optional Supplies
Heat mat
Grow lights

You can purchase kits that have seedling flats and covers that fit, or get creative with clear boxes from salads or even cut-open soda bottles covered with plastic wrap. Fill the tray with pre-moistened seed-starting mix, not potting soil. This lightweight mix is sterile and specially formulated to encourage easy, problem-free germination. Plant the seeds according to instructions, and water the seeds in the soil, taking care not to wash them away. You don't have to use a heat mat, but using one will result in faster germination and growth.

Keep the seeds covered with plastic until they sprout, then hang grow lights 2 inches above the heads of the seedlings. As the plants grow, move the lights up so that they are no more than 2 inches above the plants. Keep the seedling mix moist, but not soggy. Damping off (which looks like rotting or wilting of new seedlings) is a problem when seeds stay too wet and cold while germinating. When plants have three sets of leaves, you can transplant to a 4-inch pot.

Planting Transplants Outdoors

Plant transplants outside according to the spacing the fully grown plants will need. Plant so that the soil line of the hole and the soil line of the transplant are exactly the same. There are a few exceptions, and they are covered under the individual plant profiles. Before planting any transplants outside, prepare them by hardening them off.

Hardening Off before Planting Out

Vegetable transplants grown inside a greenhouse (or your house) need to be hardened off (acclimated to the change in temperature and light) before they're planted outside. Even if you buy plants that were sitting outside at a garden center, it's a good idea to harden them off before planting. For all you know, the plants were taken from the greenhouse, loaded on a truck, and brought to the garden center on the same day you bought them.

How to Harden Off Transplants

1. Place plants in a sheltered location such as a porch or patio for the day, and bring them in at night. Do this for three or four days.
2. Next, leave them outside all day and night in the protected location. Do this for about a week. Don't forget to water while you're doing this!
3. Finally, move the plants from the sheltered location to a more exposed location (next to the garden). Leave them there for three or four days.
4. Plant your plants in the garden early in the day, when they have ample time in sunlight to recover from the inevitable damage to their roots. If you have a cloudy day to plant in, even better.

Harden off plants by setting them on your porch or patio during the day and bringing them in at night until they are acclimated to outside conditions.

Planting Seeds Outdoors

The key to success with seeds outdoors is to pay attention to them. Seeds have to stay moist while they are germinating. If the tiny baby seedlings dry out, they will die—they have no reserves to draw on.

Take the Temperature

Before planting seeds outside, measure the temperature of the soil to make sure it is warm or cool enough. Lettuce, for example, needs soil temperatures of 70°F to 80°F.

Sow According to Finished Spacing and Germination Rates

Seed packets will have instructions to sow "thickly" (lettuce) or "thinly" (carrots, radishes). Usually these instructions correspond to germination rates. Radishes have a high germination rate, meaning that almost all of the seeds that you plant will sprout. Lettuce has a fairly high germination rate, but you want to grow lots of small leaf lettuce plants in a small space to encourage fast, leggy, tender growth. The more closely you can plant

Seedlings are fragile when they first sprout. Keep them moist but not soaking wet.

according to the finished spacing requirements, the fewer seeds you'll waste, and the less time you'll spend thinning.

Cover Your Seeds

Seedling mix isn't just for indoor plants. If the soils are too cool for a warm-season crop, cover them with nice dark seedling mix. This mix will stay loose and resist soil crusting, making it easier for the seeds to sprout.

If you are starting your cool-season garden and the soils are still warm, cover the seeds with a nice light-colored sand. I have a bucket of white play sand for just this use. Don't use too much or the neighborhood kitties may visit you.

Check Seedlings and Water Frequently

Seeds need to stay moist but not soaking wet. Check them at least twice a day. Ideally, invest in soaker hoses or a superfine hose nozzle to water with. Provide a gentle rain without washing the seedlings away. Further information about watering and caring for vegetables is discussed in Chapter 5.

Container-grown trees grow best in the Southwest.

Planting the Fruit Garden

Fruit trees and shrubs are a more permanent part of the landscape. Once you plant a tree, you're not going to move it. Thus it is important to plant fruit trees and shrubs correctly to avoid long-term problems.

In the southwest, you will want to select fruit plants that are container-grown, not bare-root or balled-and-burlapped. Those last two rarely thrive here. You will plant your fruit trees and shrubs the same way you'd plant a landscape tree or shrub.

Place the tree in the hole and adjust the hole depth so that the plant is level with or about 1 inch higher than it was planted in the nursery to allow for settling of soil. Use a shovel handle laid across the hole to help determine the proper depth.

How to Plant a Container-Grown Fruit Tree or Shrub

1. Use a shovel or marking paint to mark the area for the hole. The planting hole should be two to three times as wide as the container.
2. Dig the planting hole. This hole should be just as deep as the container— no deeper! **Hint:** Wet the soil the night before so that digging will go easily.
3. Set the container into the hole to check the depth. If the topsoil level in the container is lower than the soil line around the edge of the planting hole, add some soil back into the hole. You never want the crown of the tree (the part where the tree trunk meets the tree roots) to be below the soil line.
4. Take the plant out of the container, and place it in the hole. Check before you backfill the soil to make sure branches are not heading straight toward an obstacle (wall, driveway, another tree).
5. Fill in around the tree with a blend of the soil that you removed from the planting hole and compost. Fifty percent of each is fine. This is to encourage the roots out of the perfect nursery soil and into something closely approximating the yard soil they are going to have to get used to. Do not add fertilizer.

Fill the hole with loose soil and tamp down to ensure good contact between the soil and the roots.

6. Water the plant right away (before you plant another). This helps seal the soil around the roots and remove large air pockets.
7. Remove any nursery stake. This is in the pot to help protect the leader in transit. Most new fruit trees don't need to be staked unless they're in areas prone to heavy winds.
8. Some books advocate mulching newly planted trees. In our dry climate this can be a source of problems. If it needs mulch it is mentioned in the plant profile.

Establishing Newly Planted Fruits

Plan to water newly planted fruits every day, if not twice a day, for at least two weeks. This is what they are accustomed to in the nursery. Slowly wean them to every other day and eventually once a week during establishment. Be sure the water goes into the soil as deeply as their roots are. Trees and shrubs may take three years to become fully established in their new home, so continue to monitor your plants for signs that they need water. Fully established trees may eventually need water only once per month.

CHAPTER 5

GROWING YOUR GARDEN

Once you have started building your soil, and your seeds and seedlings are planted, the maintenance begins. Throughout the year and the growing seasons, you'll need to keep your plants producing prolifically by staying on top of these garden-maintenance tasks:

Watering

Thinning

Pinching

Weeding

Mulching

Staking and Trellising

Fertilizing

Controlling Pests

Harvesting

Soil Conditioning

Succession Planting

Mulching a vegetable garden with straw helps the soil retain moisture.

This garden was thinned when plants were smaller to allow for adequate space for the vegetables to grow and spread out.

WATERING TOOLS

You will need to water your garden. A good investment for the long-term viability of your garden water system are two common irrigation devices. First, a pressure regulator to bring garden pressure to 20 psi (pounds per square inch). House water pressure may be as high as 65 psi. This can ruin the lining of even top quality garden hoses. Second, on the pipes right next to the pressure regulator, install an irrigation filter. Made of fine mesh, it captures the microgrit common in Southwestern water. Clean it out every six months. Finally, many communities have laws that require backflow-prevention devices on all outside lines. Purchase a top quality one and add it to the array here. Avoid the tap-end types that wear out yearly.

Garden hose

A The garden hose is your main tool for watering plants. It's worth the money to buy a top quality 50-foot, heavy-duty, no-kink hose (or two).

Soaker hose

B Soaker hoses are porous hoses that lie in the garden and can connect to the faucet via irrigation line or garden hose. Made of fabric or plastic, the sewn fabric ones have a longer life in our Southwestern sunlight. Soakers can also be buried so that the water is delivered where the plants need it—at the roots.

Microdrip line

C This type of drip line is ideal for the vegetable garden. Made of ¼-inch flexible plastic, it has drip emitters built into the line at 6-inch intervals. It can be connected to a water source via irrigation line or garden hose. A tad more expensive than soaker hoses, but I like the long-term durability. Buy some ¼-inch connectors when you buy your microdrip line because when you accidentally cut it with a spade it can be repaired easily. (This is not an option with soaker hoses.)

Watering wand

D Young or old, a watering wand makes watering fun, and easy. The long rigid pipe lets you reach over head to hanging pots, over rows, or down, to water near the base of a plant without bending over.

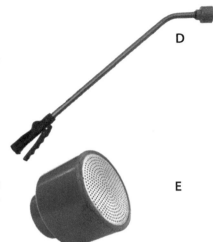

D

Rain head

E Also called a water breaker, this is used on the end of a watering wand or hose to disperse the flow of water so that it is gentler and less likely to disrupt soil, seeds, and delicate seedlings.

E

Life extenders for watering tools

F Two other tools to keep on hand are Teflon pipe tape and ample hose washers. If you use Teflon tape on all your hose threads the caliche that forms in your watering devices will be less likely to weld them shut. With desert heat, mountain cold, and alkaline water, hose washers last about six months before they start to leak. Replace as needed.

HAND TOOLS

Gloves (not pictured)

A Invest in good garden gloves. They can help you grip tools and reduce hand fatigue. Top quality gloves that fit well are worth every penny.

Trowel

B

B Small and very practical, hand trowels are used for planting, weeding, harvesting, smacking scorpions, etc. Heavy duty solid metal ones with a coated handle are best in our climate. If you tend to lose tools, buy a bunch of cheap plastic ones and scatter them all over the yard.

Soil knife

C One side of the blade is sharpened; the other is serrated like a saw. Handy for planting, digging weeds, and cutting through roots. A soil knife is a useful version of a trowel.

C

D

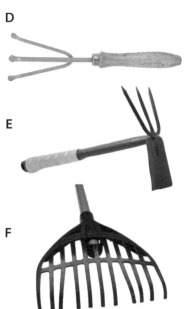

Cultivator

D The teeth, or shanks, of this tool help mix the soil, either before planting (to aerate the soil and prepare a smooth, loose seedbed) or after the crop is in (to kill weeds).

E

Hoe/cultivator

E This combo tool is especially handy for weeding and planting because sometimes you need a hoe and sometimes you need a cultivator. Sharpen the edge when it gets dull.

F

Hand rake

F For a small garden, or succession planting, a small rake allows you to move mulch in a small space. It also helps rake around shrubs.

STAND-UP TOOLS

I call them this because you stand up to use these tools. Handles can be straight or ergonomically curved, have handgrips on the end or not, and may be coated with specific compounds for easy gripping. Handles all have issues in our low humidity. Wood dries out, fiberglass frays, plastic cracks. I buy top quality wood and oil them twice a year with vegetable oil.

Shovels and spades (not pictured)

A Can you dig it? No matter the size of the blade or the length of the handle, these digging tools work best if sharpened every so often. Not knife sharp, but enough to help slide the blade into the soil.

B

Hard rake

B A hard rake has a hard head, unlike a spring or leaf rake. It is handy to rake clods and rocks from soil.

C

Hoe

C There are many different types of hoes. Hoes with narrow ends are excellent for digging planting rows. Hoes with larger, wider ends are helpful for spreading soil and mulching. These too need occasional sharpening for best usefulness.

Cultivator

D Also called a three- or four-tine claw, the tool is used to weed and cultivate between vegetable garden rows, rake mulch in narrow beds, and incorporate compost and soil amendments.

D

Garden fork or pitchfork

E Pitchforks work well to muck barns, but unless you have ideal soil, they are of limited use in the Southwest.

E

CUTTING TOOLS

The old adage, "Buy cheap, buy twice," is especially true when it comes to cutting tools. Get top quality because it is easier and far better for the plants to do it right the first time.

A

Scissors

A Really good garden scissors are more precious than gold. Use them to thin, harvest, cut twine, open bags of fertilizer, cut flowers for the home, etc. I hide mine from the hubby.

B

Hand pruners

B Hand pruners are for pruning small branches, harvesting vegetables, deadheading, and thinning fruit. Find the one just right for your hand.

Snips

C Snips are somewhere between scissors and hand pruners. Their scissor-like cutting action is offset by their spring (like hand pruners). Snips are great for thinning and deadheading.

C

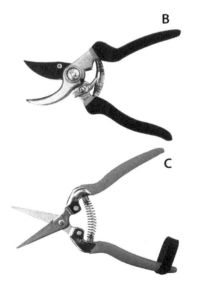

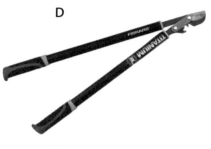

Loppers

D Loppers are basically long-handled hand pruners. Use to prune fruit branches out of arm's reach.

Pruning saw

E Used for cutting larger branches on fruit trees. If you are training your plants correctly when young, you should not need one. Varieties that fold or attach to poles are available.

PLANT SUPPORT

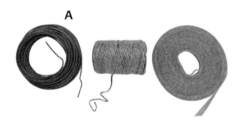

Velcro, twine, coated wire, plant tape

A All of these are handy to gently bind your plants to stakes or trellises.

Tomato cage

B Not just for tomatoes, these work well for virtually any garden plant that needs support. Especially good when summer monsoons swirl around.

Plantstakes

C You can use anything tall, skinny, and durable to stake plants. You can buy any number of common types, including metal, plastic-coated metal, bamboo stakes, cedar wood, and spiral tomato stakes. If you have some lying about, rebar works well, as the striations in the metal help keep any plant ties in place.

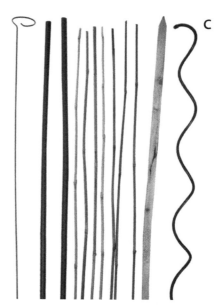

Oil wooden-handled tools with vegetable oil once or twice a year to keep them from drying out in our low humidity.

These carrot seedlings will need to be thinned to leave at least 2 inches between plants in order to harvest larger carrots later.

Garden Maintenance Activities

Watering

Watering is probably the most important single thing you can do for your garden. Vegetables and fruits only produce well if they are not stressed. Not enough water, too much water, or inconsistent water, and plants become stressed and can be more susceptible to pests and disease.

Watering Time

The best time to water is first thing in the morning, when plants wake up for the day. This is especially true for the warm-season garden. Many plants perform all the photosynthesis they need for the day by 10 o'clock in our brilliant sunshine, and spend the rest of the day just hanging out. Water applied at the end of the day (after work) has all night to evaporate before the plants wake up the next morning and need it.

Watering Seedlings

Seeds and seedlings are an exception to the above, they need to stay continually moist while sprouting. They don't have reserves to fall back on. If you plant seeds in the garden, check them at least twice a day to make sure their soil is moist.

Avoid watering the top of the plant. A watering wand will help apply water at the base

Watering Depth

It's better to water all plants as deeply as they need it but only as frequently as they need it. Only you can prevent your plants from becoming "sip-junkies." How deep is deep enough? What crop are you growing? Mature tomato roots grow to 2 feet (or more) underground while lettuce and other greens are generally only 1 foot deep. Plan on watering 2 feet deep for your warm-season garden, and 1 foot for the cool-season plants.

Lay a soaker hose after you plant, while the plants are still small. You can use sod staples to hold the hose in place.

Watering with Irrigation

Using irrigation or soaker hoses isn't a "fix-it and forget-it" option. You still need to monitor the plants to see if the water they need is getting there. Timers break down, hoses spring leaks, and things can clog.

WHAT IS A WEED, AND WHAT IS A SEEDLING?

Sometimes seedlings look like weeds and vice versa. Lambs quarters is a kissing cousin of spinach. Know what you're removing before you remove it.

Incidentally, young lambs quarters is not only edible but also highly palatable.

Lambs quarter can sometimes be mistaken for spinach.

Thinning

When you plant seeds, you should sow more densely than you'll need because they don't all sprout. But, this also means you will need to thin or remove some of the seedlings. This allows the remaining plants to grow to their full potential. If you don't thin root vegetables such as radishes or carrots, and larger plants such as kale, you end up with small root crops and scrawny plants. To thin without disturbing the remaining plants, use scissors to snip off seedlings at the soil level.

Pinching

A number of garden plants need their growth controlled. You need to pinch fruiting plants such as okra, tomatoes, and peppers to get fewer, larger fruits. You will need to pinch basil to encourage it to branch and produce more tasty leaves. Pinching can be done with fingers, or tools such as scissors or pruners.

Weeding

You need to get weeds out of the garden before they become large and steal the water and nutrients from your vegetables. You especially need to get weeds before they go to seed. "One year's seeding is seven years weeding." This is where you get to use your shiny new cultivator tools!

The good news is that many common garden weeds are edible. Most of them were once the staples of the Natives, and they taught the miners, trappers, cowboys, and pioneers their usefulness. In the age of supermarket vegetables, most people avoid miners lettuce and lambs quarters, but they are both lovely additions to the salad bowl or cook pot. Do take the time to properly identify any volunteer plants before you eat them. Your Cooperative Extension Office and local native plant society has appropriate information for your area.

Mulching

A layer of mulch in the vegetable garden will save you much water and much time spent weeding. It is amazing the difference that a thick, 3-inch layer of mulch will make.

Mulch needs to lie above the soil and not start to decompose excessively as it protects. It also needs to allow oxygen to get through to the roots, and for the warm-season garden, it should not add any more heat to the soil. Also, when mulching around your plants, avoid mounding the mulch up on the stems of the plants, since it can cause rot and/or harbor insect pests.

Good materials for vegetable garden mulch include:

Shredded leaves
Wheat or oat straw
Shredded hardwood mulch
Shredded newspaper or junk mail

Avoid hay and Bermudagrass clippings since they bring weed problems with them.

Staking and Trellising

Certain vegetables need a helping hand to grow upright and reach the light; these you will stake or trellis. Then there are those with brittle stems that can't support the weight of their fruits; they need help too. The plant profiles cover which ones need help.

A word from experience: It is much easier to place the plant supports as you plant. Place trellises before you plant and cages right after. Trying to wrestle a large, vining plant into a cage or support after it has started growing is frustrating and can harm the plant you are trying to help.

When tying a plant to a stake, line the stake up to the main stem of the plant. Then tie the plant to the stake, but never tie the string so tight that the plant is smashed against the stake.

Sidedress plants with organic fertilizers (sprinkle them on the soil alongside the plants) every few weeks to help your vegetables thrive better.

Fertilizing

Plants make all of their own food. That is what photosynthesis is all about. To feed themselves, plants need certain elements and minerals out of the soil. That is what fertilizer is all about. People speak of fertilizer as "plant food," an oxymoron and wrong to boot.

Fertilizers add the essential macronutrients that plants need for life: nitrogen, phosphorous, and potassium, or by chemical symbols—N, P, and K. You can purchase fertilizer in more forms than you can shake a stick at, and they come with a bewildering variety of labels. By government mandate, the N-P-K amounts will be listed, and in that order. These three macronutrients are needed in specific parts of the plant for the main processes that occur there.

Different Types of Fertilizer

For optimal health and production, vegetables and fruits need ample fertilizer. Different plants have different requirements (see the plant profiles). When possible, use organic fertilizers. Your garden will benefit in the long run. Think of synthetic fertilizer as a candy bar—it provides quick nutrients to the plants, but the effects are fleeting, plus synthetic fertilizers may include harmful salts that can build up in the soil over time. Which fertilizer you purchase is something you have to choose for yourself. Consider your tolerance for fussing with application methods, your desire to nurture your soil over time, and your wallet.

Fertilizer is sold to be placed onto the soil or used as a foliar spray, for application to the leaves of plants. Avoid foliar sprays as they have a tendency to burn plants in our arid climate.

Fertilizer is offered in three main forms—liquid, powder, or granular. Liquid fertilizer is mixed with water (in a can or bucket) and watered into the soil. Powdered and granular (slow-release) forms are generally spread directly onto the soil. Many of our Southwestern birds will eat the dry fertilizers, thinking it is a new form of seed, and it can kill them. Consider dissolving powdered and granular fertilizers and watering them into the soil.

Less is More for Fertilizers

Follow the label directions! Err on the side of caution when using fertilizers. Too much can easily kill the plant you wish to help, even if it is an organic fertilizer. It is always safe to use half as much twice as often.

Nutrient Deficiencies

If your plant leaves are turning unusual colors for the species (purple, yellow), they might have nutrient deficiencies. Nutrient deficiencies are tough for the novice gardener but it's usually possible to diagnose a nutrient deficiency with a careful look at the plant.

The diagram below shows the symptoms caused by the most common nutrient deficiencies.

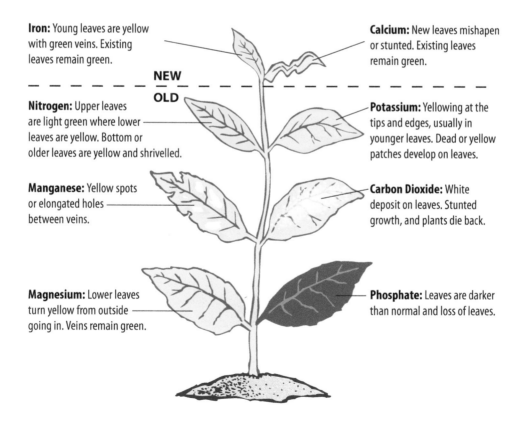

Iron: Young leaves are yellow with green veins. Existing leaves remain green.

Calcium: New leaves mishapen or stunted. Existing leaves remain green.

NEW
OLD

Nitrogen: Upper leaves are light green where lower leaves are yellow. Bottom or older leaves are yellow and shrivelled.

Potassium: Yellowing at the tips and edges, usually in younger leaves. Dead or yellow patches develop on leaves.

Manganese: Yellow spots or elongated holes between veins.

Carbon Dioxide: White deposit on leaves. Stunted growth, and plants die back.

Magnesium: Lower leaves turn yellow from outside going in. Veins remain green.

Phosphate: Leaves are darker than normal and loss of leaves.

Controlling Pests

There is nothing more discouraging than carefully tending your garden only to see it destroyed by pests. Each edible plant has its own pest problems, which are outlined in the plant profiles. Compiling a chart for the entire Southwest is well beyond the scope of this book. But, your local Cooperative Extension Service has a booklet on the common garden pests for your specific area. This will help you identify any problem and offer solutions. Before you take action, it's important to understand pests, pesticides, and their relationship to your garden.

Pests: A Fact of Life

There are insects and animals and bacteria and fungi and even viruses everywhere, eating everything, including each other. That's just how the world is. Everything is food for something else. As my mentor quoted, "Every flea has a flea on his back to bite him, and so on and so on, *ad infinitum*." Your garden is a very specific ecosystem, and ecosystems have their own system of checks and balances. If you choose to use chemicals to control certain pests (even if they are organic chemicals), you will mess with the checks and balances, and that can have consequences.

Diversity Is Key

I have not used pesticides for years. How do I avoid using them? I have a wide diversity of native and non-native fruits, vegetables, flowers, trees, shrubs, and herbs in my yard. This biologically diverse garden and landscape supports a wide diversity of beneficial insects that prey on harmful insects. I have also learned to have a tolerance for pest activity. You have to have many aphids to feed a hungry praying mantis. One or two aphids are just part of life.

Garden design or overall layout matters in terms of pest control, too. Clumping all similar vegetables in one big block makes it easier for the first pest to find them, and then easier for baby pests to dine on and spread throughout. Try planting only a few of each edible at each place throughout the garden. The pests might find only one clump and stick with it, allowing the other plants to thrive.

Beneficial Insects

You can encourage beneficial insects, such as praying mantis, ladybugs, lacewings, soldier beetles, wasps, spiders, and others, to live in your yard by limiting the use of broad-spectrum biocidal chemicals that kill everything, and by growing a diverse landscape. Remember, chemicals that kill everything kill the insects that are working for you, too.

Integrated Pest Management (IPM)

This type of garden and landscape care means you have to step back and take a look at the big picture. Integrate your approach to garden care.

There are four "pillars" to IPM.

Set action thresholds: Decide what amount of damage you're willing to live with.

Monitor and identify pests: Most insects you see are not garden pests. Early detection of true pests leads to early action before much damage can be done.

Prevention: Do what you can to prevent pest and disease problems. Plant resistant varieties, use barriers to keep pests away, and provide good culture—the best care possible so plants can withstand problems.

Control: After all of the other steps, you can decide how to control pests. Controls can be organic or synthetic, involve treating the pests, or removing the affected plants.

Organic versus Synthetic Controls

There's a misconception that if you use an organic pesticide, you're not putting yourself or your pets or your plants in any danger. False! Organic pesticides made from naturally occurring ingredients can be just as deadly as pesticides synthesized in a lab. When deciding to use a biocide to control weeds, pests, or diseases, always read the label and follow all the instructions—including those for dosage, protective equipment, re-entry timing, and harvest.

Controlling Non-Insect Pests

Pack rats, mice, rabbits, various species of squirrels, raccoons, javalina, and even deer are all mammalian problems in the edible garden. Then there are the birds. The most effective way to control these pests is with barriers. Fencing, repellents, and netting are just about the only way to keep these pests out of the garden. Plants that especially suffer bird predation are mentioned in the plant profiles.

One example of IBM is to encourage predator insects like the praying mantis.

Some vegetables are easier to harvest with scissors, so you don't yank the plant out of the ground. Here, the gardener is using scissors to cut the pepper. If she twisted the pepper off the plant, she could break or damage the rest of the plant.

Harvesting

When to harvest? It's easier to tell when some fruits and vegetables are ready than others. Information about harvesting each plant type is found in the individual plant profiles.

Here are some general tips about harvesting:

- Days to maturity are printed on the seed packets for two reasons. First, to let folks know if they have enough frost-free days to grow the vegetable. Second, to let you know when to get out the harvest basket.
- With very few exceptions, mama plant will release her fruits into your hand with a gentle tug when they are at their peak of flavor. Let fruits ripen on the plant for as long as possible. If you pick a tomato green, it may turn red and soften, but it won't be as tasty.
- Use hand pruners or scissors to harvest eggplants, peppers, and other fruits that don't easily snap off. You don't want to yank the plant out of the ground.
- Harvest in the morning when everything has the highest water content. Food will last longer before eating and will be fresher and crisper.

■ Learn how big the finished product is supposed to be. If the eggplant is supposed to be 1 inch wide and 4 inches long, but you let it grow to be 4 inches wide and 1 foot long, it will not taste very good.

Soil Conditioning

Soil conditioning is an ongoing process, working to help keep the soil optimal for the fruits and vegetables you wish to produce. There are two forces at work to get Southwestern soil out of condition. Our water and subsoils are alkaline, but plants prefer to grow in neutral or slightly acidic soils. Even if you plant in potting soil, every time you water your plants, you slowly tip the soil toward the alkaline side of the scales. Soil pH is not the only issue. The organic matter (compost) you add to the soil to improve porosity and water-holding ability breaks down over time and must be replaced.

Every time you harvest your vegetables and remove the crop, it is a good idea to add compost to the soil and mix it in. You may also add fertilizer, such as steer manure, but compost is needed as a soil conditioner.

To add compost to fruit trees and shrubs, plan on treating one-third to one-half of the plant each year. Rake or hoe away the top inch of soil. You can go deeper if you aren't hitting any roots. Add a ¾-inch layer of compost to the hole and cover the last ¼ inch with the soil you removed. Water well to help pull the nutrients and natural acids down into the soil.

You can toss used coffee grounds around your garden at any time and they help condition the soil as well. We keep a 5-gallon bucket in the laundry room and slowly fill it with grounds each morning. If you use paper coffee filters you may prefer to compost your coffee before adding to the garden.

Succession Planting

Do you have a small yard, raised bed, and not enough space to grow all you want? Common complaints here in caliche-land. Succession planting is key. Carefully plan your garden not just in space but over time. It takes a little practice and thinking ahead. You also have to be ready, willing, and able to pull out plants that are still producing. With some plants you can do this over a few weeks. Pull out every other arugula plant and put in eggplant seedlings. As the seedlings grow and the arugula gets tough and bitter, it is easier to remove the last of that crop. At the other end of the season, plant seedlings of autumn bok choy or kale between the eggplants; a little shade won't hurt them when they are young and the summer heat is still on. The young plants will need more sun about the time the last of the eggplant fades. Don't forget to condition the soil before you plant! Even a handful of compost will help the soil.

PART II

FRUIT & VEGETABLE PROFILES

In these pages you may encounter some fruits and vegetables you may have never heard of before. That is because our Southwest is such a unique place, and some pretty unique plants live here—some of them quite tasty. Not only tasty, but since they are from here they are easy to grow here!

Western elderberry (*Sambucus caerulea*)

This section is arranged into two chapters. Chapter 6 covers fruits and nuts, mostly growing on trees, and in a few cases, shrubs. These are plants that you will maintain as part of the landscape of your yard, not in a cultivated vegetable garden. Chapter 7 covers vegetables and herbs and is further broken down into cool and warm seasons in the garden. When you get to warm-season vegetables you may find many things you think of as fruit, like watermelon, but technically a tomato is a fruit as well. If it has seeds, it is a fruit. Since these fruiting vegetables and fruit have many of the same planting and care needs, they are together in one chapter.

CHAPTER 6

FRUIT & NUT GARDENING

Fruit production in the Southwest is highly dependent on where precisely you live. Think of the difference between Santa Fe and Albuquerque, relatively close as the crow flies, but very different climates. Each Southwestern state has such examples, like Reno and Las Vegas, or Flagstaff and Phoenix.

Citrus trees can be grown in the warmer areas of the Southwest.

In the three states covered by this book, we can grow various tropical fruits such as avocado, banana, carob, dates, and on through the alphabet. In the cool country of those same states we can grow apples, blackberries, cherries, etc., including persimmons, pawpaws, and hardy kiwi. Sadly, dealing with each and every one of these specific fruits with their narrow growth zones is beyond the scope of this book (but I have hopes for a sequel that will go into details!).

In this chapter, we will focus on the fruits that can be most easily grown in the most highly populated areas covered by this book. But don't let this limit you! Your local County Cooperative Extension Service is there to help you get started with an edible landscape.

Experiment if you want. If you are a knowledgeable gardener, or have a friendly neighbor growing some of the ones on this list, do try them out. Who knows—you may already be growing some since some are commonly used as landscape plants. Here are some more fruit to consider, depending on where you live: akebia, American chestnut, Arizona fan palm, aronia, avocado, Barbados cherry, barrel cactus, beauty berry, buffalo berry, Capulin cherry, choke cherry, Cornelian cherry, currant, desert hackberry, dragon fruit, gogi berry, gooseberry, goumi, grape, guava (strawberry), guava (tropical), hazelnut, honey berry, jaboticaba, lichi, maypop, mespilus (medlar), mulberry, nopalito, passion flower, persimmon (Texas), persimmon (northern), pine nut, prickly pear, seaberry, strawberry, walnut, and white sapote, etc.

Planting

Fruits that live for many years, as opposed say to watermelon, are generally woody in nature. With their wood, these fruits can grow into large trees, or, at the very least, sizable shrubs. Since they are going to be in your landscape for quite a long time, it is very important to plant them in just the right place, and to plant them correctly. Care is critical! Care includes proper pruning, fertilizing, watering, and cultural practices. Care of these long lasting garden members is important for fruit production, and also to maintain the value of the plant itself and thus ultimately the value of your home. If you are an indifferent gardener, flip to the vegetable chapter and you and your wallet will thank me.

Chill Hours

Many of the trees we grow for fruit need to have some time to "chill out." Termed "chill hours," it is defined as a specific number of cumulative hours of temperatures lower than 45°F. Some of these trees are even evergreen, like olives, but for good fruit set, they need their accumulated hours of chilling weather.

Mature seed pods hang from the branches of a mesquite tree.

It is important to know the chilling requirements of any fruit and nut trees you plan on planting because inadequate chilling causes poor, if any, crop. Thus, knowing your local chill hours is helpful for selecting the right tree. Some of the fruits discussed here originated in cooler climates, like apples and apricots, and they will require a greater number of chill hours per winter in order to set fruit. While there are low-chill varieties of some species, you will need to match the number of chill hours of your specific area to the chill hours of the recommended variety. You may adore Elberta peaches, but if you don't get enough chill hours, don't waste your resources—time, money, and garden space—on an Elberta peach tree.

Pollination

Plants will not produce fruit without having their flowers pollinated. A number of the fruiting plants in these pages are self-fertile, meaning their pollen is sufficient to pollinate themselves (insects may have to actually do the work). If plants are self-fertile, growing a single plant will be enough. Self-sterile plants will need a second plant of a different variety in order to set fruit. Consider how much space you have available and whether you need to plant one or two (or more) to achieve your desired results.

Fertilizer

Fertilizer is very much the same for all these fruits. As a rule of thumb, in Low, Middle and High Desert, apply a well-balanced fertilizer three times per year: Memorial Day, Fourth of July, and Labor Day. In the Cool Highlands and Cold Mountain Region, omit the last, or fertilize on the first of August. Specific additional fertilizer, generally a bloom fertilizer or a fruiting fertilizer, both high in phosphorous, may be required at other times by specific plants. A few of the plants in this chapter have highly specific mineral requirements, but this is generally not an issue in our mineral-rich Southwestern soils.

Pruning

In all cases, you should train a young plant and then pretty much leave it alone. Pruning books will show you how to take off large limbs, but if you are pruning correctly, you should never need to take off anything larger than what you can do with hand clippers, or at most, loppers.

Here in the Southwest, we have a number of trees that purposefully grow arching branches to shade their trunks, and if you prune away too much of their self-made shade you can damage or even kill the tree. Citrus bark is especially susceptible to sunburn in our searing Southwestern summer sun. Dead wood and branches rubbing on one another should be removed at any stage of a tree's life, but at the recommended time for pruning.

Lost Leaders

Occasionally a plant from the nursery may have lost its dominant leader and the tree will grow wide not tall. This is because several branches are fighting with each other to be the new leader, and the hormone messages they are all sending out make it hard for the tree to grow tall. Look into the center of the tree and spot the two or three branches that are fighting for dominance. Simply select the one that is as close to upright and as centered as possible and clip off the others. Even if the trunk currently appears to have an "S" curve, within two to three years you will not even see the wound and the trunk will be straight.

Fruit Thinning

It may seem odd to thin out what appear to be perfectly good fruit. But some fruit trees have been so bred to produce that they can overdo it, and the crop is heavier than the limbs can withstand. To ensure good fruit size, return bloom for the following year, and to prevent tree breakage, it is necessary to thin the fruit. In general thin your fruit after the natural "June drop" (which can happen in May). Species that require it will be noted.

CITRUS *(Citrus* species,
Fortunella species, and hybrids)

Key lime tree

If you include citrus species, varieties, and hybrids, there are well over 1,500 names out there—and covering them all is well beyond the scope of this book! But, here are some general tips and information to help get your started.

Tropical in origin, most citrus do not take kindly to freezing temperatures. Over the centuries, the human race has bred a few varieties that are hardy to 10°F, but they are the exception rather than the rule. When deciding to plant citrus, look at how cold it will get in your yard, factor in how much fussing you want to do over the plant(s), and decide what your family will eat. You can grow at least some citrus in the ground in the Desert zones, but in the upper elevations you will need to grow citrus in containers and bring them indoors in winter.

If you live in a cool area, planting citrus near a south or east facing wall or near a swimming pool will help protect them somewhat in winter. But, in summer, those sites put massive heat stress on a plant. A warm winter morning wall with afternoon shade is ideal. Mature size is also quite important to consider before you plant. Some varieties of grapefruit trees can easily reach 30 feet tall and wide. Use citrus grafted on special roots called "dwarfing rootstock" for smaller yards or growing in containers.

■ *Citrus Cold Hardiness*

All citrus will freeze. Cold hardiness refers to leaf or wood and tree tolerance before damage occurs. Citrus fruit itself easily freezes if it drops to 32°F and lasts for more than a few hours.

The official temperature in your city may be very different from what a tree in your yard experiences. If you live near the base of a mountain, cold air falls and your yard can freeze without posted frost warnings. Microclimate is extremely important to ensure citrus success.

Rootstocks

Citrus are usually grafted onto a disease-resistant dwarfing rootstock. The most commonly used rootstock is sour or trifoliate orange. If your tree freezes and the only part that comes back is below the graft union, you now have a sour orange tree. At least sour oranges are good for making marmalade (and you can get into a great deal of trouble using them as ammunition in "Capture the Flag").

Recommended Varieties

Citrus greening, Huanglongbing (HLB), is of great concern in our area as it can devastate the orchards forever and do billions of dollars in damage. Please purchase your citrus only from a certified and licensed nursery. If you see yellow splotches on your citrus leaves contact your Cooperative Extension Service.

The citrus listed below start with the most cold hardy and go to the least. I am referring to the cold tolerance of the plant. The fruit itself easily freezes anytime temperatures drop below 32°F for several hours.

UNSHIU OR SATSUMA TANGERINE (*Citrus unshiu*): Also called cold-hardy mandarin. The most cold-hardy citrus you can grow, hardy to 15°F to 10°F, used for eating. Try these varieties: 'Ten Degree Tangerine', and 'Owari.'

CALAMONDIN (*Citrus mitis*): An excellent container plant. Grown in the ground, they are hardy to 15°F. Small decorative fruit generally used for culinary purposes.

KUMQUAT (*Fortunella* species): A good citrus choice for smaller yards or containers. Hardy to 15°F to 20°F. 'Meiwa' kumquat (*Fortunella crassifolia*) is a sweeter species with a round shape.

'NAGAMI' KUMQUAT (*Fortunella margarita*): Has oval form and thin skin. People tend to eat them whole. 'Changshou' descended from 'Nagami', is a dwarf variety from Japan, excellent in containers, featuring sweet flesh and juice.

SOUR ORANGE (*Citrus trifoliata*): Hardy to 20°F. Often used as rootstock for other citrus. Fruit used for culinary purposes, including marmalade and a lemonade-like drink.

'MEYER' LEMON (*Citrus × meyeri*): Native to China, a cross between a true lemon and either a mandarin or common orange. Hardy to 20°F, used for culinary purposes, can be grown in containers. Also try 'Improved Meyer.'

TANGERINE (*Citrus tangerina*): Will require cross-pollination by another tangerine or tangelo. Hardy to 26°F. Used for eating. For our soils consider: 'Algerian', 'Dandy', 'Fairchild', 'Fremont', 'Honey', and 'Kinnow.'

Tangelos, tangors, and honeybells are miscellaneous hybrids of the tangerine, in general hardy to 28°F, mostly used for eating. They will require cross-pollination by another tangerine or tangelo. 'Minneola' is popular for both eating and juice, or try 'Orlando.'

MANDARIN ORANGE (*Citrus reticulata*) AND HYBRIDS: Hardy to 26°F to 32°F. Used for eating, fruit is smaller than oranges, and easily peeled like a tangerine. Consider 'California Honey', 'Clementine', 'Gold Nugget', 'Kishu', 'Murcott', 'Tahoe Gold', 'Tango', or 'Yosemite Gold'.

SWEET ORANGE (*Citrus sinensis*): Includes navel and blood orange. Hardy to about 28°F, good for eating and juicing. Sweet: 'Arizona Sweet', 'Diller', 'Hamlin', and 'Macetera.' Navel: 'Cara Cara' and 'Don Shaw.' Blood: 'Burgundy', 'Moro', 'Ruby', and 'Sanguinelli.'

GRAPEFRUIT (*Citrus × paradisi*): Hardy to around 28°F, grapefruits need ample long hot days in summer to mature the fruit. Consider 'Redblush', 'Marsh White', 'Rio Red', 'Star Ruby', and 'Rio Star.' 'Oroblanco' can be grown in containers.

PUMELO OR SHADDOCK (*Citrus maxima*): Hardy to around 28°F, pumelos need ample long hot days in summer to mature the fruit. Prefer higher humidity than grapefruit and require more water.

LIME, RANGPUR OR LEMANDARIN (*Citrus × limonia*): Hybrid between mandarin and lemon, with orange peel and flesh, not a true lime. Hardy to 28°F. Used for culinary purposes.

LEMON, TRUE LEMON (*Citrus × limon*): Hardy to 30°F, used for culinary purposes. 'Butwal', 'Lisbon', and 'Ponderosa' do well in the Southwest. 'Variegated Pink' can be grown in containers.

LEMON, MEDITERRANEAN SWEET (*Citrus limetta*): Has fruit shaped like a tangerine. Hardy to 32°F. 'Femminello Santa Teresa', 'Genoa', 'Limonero Fino', or 'Villa Franca.'

LIME, KIEFFIR OR INDONESIAN (*Citrus hystrix*): Hardy to 32°F. Leaves are used for culinary purposes. Bumpy fruit has little juice and is generally not used. Can be grown in containers.

LIME, MEXICAN, KEY, BARTENDER'S OR WEST INDIAN (*Citrus aurantifolia*): Hardy to 32°F. Often grown on their own rootstock, may resprout after a bad freeze.

LIME, TAHITI, PERSIAN, OR BEARSS (*Citrus × latifolia*): Hardy to 32°F. Can be grown in containers.

CITRON OR ETROG (*Citrus medica*): Hardy to 32°F. Consider 'Ha'Eretz' an etrog form or 'Buddha's Hand' where the fruit develops a number of "fingers." Can be grown in containers.

Kumquats tolerate colder temperatures and grow smaller than many other types of citrus.

Pollination: Most citrus are self-fertile and do not need another tree to cross-pollinate. The exception is tangerines and their kin, which do require a different variety as a pollinator.

Chill Hours: None.

◼ *Planting Citrus*

Plant citrus in the soil or in containers in early spring. Avoid planting during the heat of summer. Never plant citrus with the crown (point where trunk and roots meet) below the soil line. When in doubt, plant at exactly the same level as the plant is in the pot.

Soil: Citrus grows best in a well-drained loam soil with a pH of 6.5 to 7.5. In much of the Southwest this means adding compost to the soil on a regular basis. Planting trees in tree wells and mulching the roots with cedar bark is one good way to help citrus thrive.

■ *Maintenance*

Water: Citrus require 20 to 40 inches of water per year depending on size and species. Water should be applied to a 3-foot depth and then allowed to dry somewhat. A thick layer of cedar bark mulch will help hold in moisture, reduce weeds, help acidify the soil, and discourage pests. Keep mulch 2 to 3 inches away from the trunk to avoid disease. Renew as needed.

Fertilizer: Citrus, with its often early bloom, does well with a balanced fertilizer on three holidays discussed at the start of the chapter (Memorial Day, Fourth of July, and Labor Day). Along with these holidays, citrus appreciates some help setting fruit. Add a bloom fertilizer when the first flower buds appear. This can be followed in mid-June and mid-August with additional applications of citrus or fruiting fertilizer. A good compost applied all around the tree every spring and watered through to bring the nutrients into the soil is also ideal for long-term health and fruit production. Note that it is critical to avoid placing any organic material against the trunk itself. This can cause a number of disease issues.

Pruning: Prune only to remove dead wood or suckers sprouting below the graft union. Citrus grow best with their foliage reaching the ground, shading their roots and trunk. Avoid pruning citrus up into a lollipop shape; their trunks are especially susceptible to sun scald and wind burn, plus exposed trunks also are more susceptible to freezing. Prune if branches are rubbing each other or against buildings. After a freeze do not prune a thing until after April first. Often what you think is dead will recover.

Fruit Thinning: Citrus trees will naturally drop about half of their flowers during bloom and then another third to half of their fruits before fruits mature. That is normal unless leaves are also drooping, in which case it is a sign of stress.

Pests and Diseases: Alkaline-induced Iron Chlorosis is a very common problem with citrus in our alkaline soils. The leaves turn yellow, while leaf veins remain green. (In HLB there are splotches not patterns.) This is not a disease, rather an inability to pick up the iron that is present in our soil. Treat by acidifying soil. Give your citrus used coffee grounds every morning (or as often as possible). Alternatively treat once per week with ¼ cup white vinegar in 4 gallons of water until leaves get better. Then do it once a month throughout the warm season.

Gummosis is the term for when sap curdles and bubbles out of damaged areas on the trunk and branches. The bark generally gets damaged by sunburn or mulch against the trunk. Remove the curdles and paint with a 10 percent solution of potassium permanganate. Repeat as needed.

Insects don't want to kill their food source, thus their harm is generally tolerable. The most common caterpillar is the dog face, named for the butterfly. The caterpillar looks like a bird dropping. Most homeowners don't ever notice them, but if you do and they bother you, pluck them off with tweezers, avoiding the red horns they stick out at you, and drop in a bucket of soapy water.

Thrips and aphids suck the sap of young leaves and twigs in spring. Rinse off with a blast from a garden hose. They can cause leaf curl, which is unsightly. Once they are gone, it is too late to treat.

Potted citrus indoors may get scale. Resolve by placing the plant outside, once it is warm enough. Natural predators will show up to eat the scale. That said, place infested trees well away from your other fruit trees.

■ *Harvest & Storage*

Skin color is no indicator of ripeness. Mamma citrus tree will release her baby ripe fruit into your hand when you gently tug on it. Some varieties ripen slowly over time, weeks and even months (I know one grapefruit tree that offers its fruit from January through July). Depending on variety, expect fruit from late fall (tangerines) through early spring (oranges).

ELDERBERRY
(*Sambucus mexicanus* and *Sambucus cereulea*)

The flowers of elderberry can be made into champagne or wine, but you will get less fruit, if you pick the flowers.

Various species of elderberry are found around the globe in the Northern Hemisphere, and here in the Southwest we are lucky enough to have two species of our very own. What a delightful plant this is, providing soothing summer shade, decorative wood with many uses, and a delightfully tasty and health-giving fruit. The flowers, rich in nectar, can be used to make elderberry champagne or delicious elderberry fritters. This native, deciduous tree can reach 20 to 30 feet high, spreading to 20 feet wide when grown in full sun in average, well-drained soil and with ample moisture.

Wildlife prize the berries, as the fruit is sweet and both the berry and the seed are rich in waxes and oils. Since I want to share my yard with wildlife, I harvest what I need, process the fruit, then put the seed pulp back out by the trees for the wildlife to feast upon. And yes, it does stain the flagstones for a while, but a few good rains and the stains wash away. A small price to pay to watch the cardinals and phainopepla cavort. The insectivorous birds come down to check out the action and help clean up any insects eating the pulp.

■ *Recommended Varieties*

Low, Middle, and High Desert: Can grow *Sambucus mexicanus*, a plant that is generally more tree-like.

High Desert, Cool Highlands, and Cold Mountains: Grow the more shrubby *Sambucus cereulea*. Avoid the blue-berried *Sambucus canadensis*, native to "Back East," since it does not thrive in our alkaline soils.

Caution: All species of *Sambucus* have more or less edible berries, but some of the wild species can be toxic without special preparation. Buy from a reputable source.

Pollination: Plant it and they will come. Butterflies love the broad flat cluster of tiny flowers as do many other pollinators. Cross-pollination is not required.

Chill Hours: Likely, but no good information is available.

■ *Planting*

Avoid planting in midsummer in all zones. Ideally plant in fall or early spring. A handful of seeds, well-buried and kept moist, will quickly grow into a fruit-producing tree.

Soil: Be sure the soil is well-drained, not clay. Plants do best with a pH of 6.2 to 7.2.

■ *Maintenance*

Water: 20 to 30 inches of rain per year, every two weeks in summer. Not a xeriscape plant per say, but can tolerate drying between watering. Prefers dry roots during winter dormancy.

Fertilizer: Apply a bloom food three times per year, as the plant first breaks dormancy in spring, midsummer, and one month before first frost in your area.

Pruning: If you must, prune when plants are dormant. After shaping young plants, none is required.

Pests: There are few known pests of the elderberry, which is why this is a good starter plant for the beginning gardener.

■ *Harvest & Storage*

Elderberry syrup and jam and jelly, oh yum! You can harvest elder flowers and dry them for later use. Fresh flowers are high in sugar and make a nice wine or champagne. By far the most common use of elder is the berries. Harvest by cutting the stem below the cluster. Berries can be dried for later use or pressed for juice. (If you have a juice press, great.) The juice will last about two weeks under refrigeration.

Most commonly the berries are made into a syrup. Heat them gently with water to soften the flesh. Strain out the seeds and pulp as you would to make jelly. Add honey or sugar, generally in the ratio of two parts juice to one part sweetener. You can store this in the refrigerator for two to three months, or further preserve by canning.

Figs taste best when allowed to fully ripen on the tree.

FIG *(Ficus carica)*

Figs are one of the easiest fruit trees to grow in our area. They do well in our alkaline soils, and can quickly grow into lovely, spreading shade trees. Trees produce fruit in as little as two to three years, and thrive and produce with little effort for the next hundred years or so. Figs do not need cross-pollination, so a single tree can produce ample fruit for a household.

Fig trees can be grown throughout North America (I saw some in Quebec), but you will have to select the right variety for your area. Young plants are more tender, but mature plants are all hardy to about 10°F, especially if they are pruned as a bush and covered in winter (or grown in a pot and brought inside in winter).

Fig trees have attractive smooth pale creamy-gray bark and large bright green leaves. They are deciduous, dropping their leaves in autumn, and thus make charming shade trees for summer heat, allowing the sun in to warm your home in winter. Depending on the variety, a mature fig tree can reach 25 to 40 feet tall and spread 25 to 60 feet wide. Lucky for those of us who live on smaller home lots, fig trees can very easily be pruned to a tidy, compact form, a tiny 6 by 6 feet even, although a larger canopy will produce more fruit. Figs can be espaliered, pruned, and anchored to grow flat along a wall. Figs can also be grown as container plants, so if you are not yet in your "forever home," you can still grow your own fruit.

◼ *Recommended Varieties*

Since the trees grow so large and the native pollinators do not (yet) exist on our continent, only grow varieties of figs that do not require cross-pollination. For best results, select fig trees from nurseries in our states, preferably locally grown plants.

Low Desert: 'Kadota', 'Kino Heritage'

Middle Desert: for fresh and dried fruit: 'Black Mission', 'Kadota', 'Kino Heritage', and 'White Mission', for drying 'Conadria'

Upper Desert: for fresh and dried fruit 'Kino Heritage', 'Texas Everbearing', and the 'King' series, including 'Desert King'

Cool Highlands: 'Celeste', 'Brown Turkey', 'Brunswick', 'Greenish', 'Marseilles', and 'Magnolia'

Cold Mountains: Grow figs in containers and bring them inside in the winter. You will need to select a dwarf variety such as: 'Lattarula' or 'Stella'

Pollination: Figs do not need cross-pollination, so a single tree can produce ample fruit for a household.

Chill Hours: 50 to 100 hours, most growers consider it "few hours."

◼ *Planting*

Plant fig trees in the ground in late winter to early spring when they're dormant. Figs won't become well-established if planted during summer. Site the trees in full sun in the High Desert. In Low and Middle Desert the trees will do best with afternoon shade in summer.

Soil: Amend with ample compost and sand if necessary so soil is nutrient-rich and well-drained.

■ *Maintenance*

Water: Regular water ensures a good crop and long-term tree health. Established trees will need 30 to 40 inches of water, depending on size. Water to 3 feet deep once every two weeks in summer.

Fertilizer: Fertilize at the three standard summer holidays. The spring application should be "bloom" fertilizer, but the other two can be general purpose.

One fig tree produces enough fruit for most families, so be sure to plant a tree that doesn't require cross-pollination.

Pruning: Figs are pruned mainly to keep them from taking over the landscape. Prune figs in late winter while they are still dormant.

Pests: Figs are largely pest-free plants, making them ideal for home gardens. The biggest problem affecting figs is root-knot nematodes, generally not a problem in our soils. Purchase certified nematode-free plants and inspect the roots before planting. If the roots look knobby or knotty, do not plant, and return the fig to the nursery with proper cautions. Root-knot nematodes are hard to control once they find their way into your landscape.

■ *Harvest & Storage*

Along with the landscape benefits of fig trees, the fig fruits have many benefits. When you enjoy figs, you help yourself to a taste of health. Figs are rich in complex carbohydrates, are a good source of dietary fiber plus a wealth of essential minerals such as potassium, iron, and calcium. Indeed, a half-cup of fresh figs has as much calcium as a half-cup of milk. Dried figs are a nonfat, zero-cholesterol snack, and are deliciously portable, so they are readily available as calcium-rich snacks at home, work, play, or on the road.

Figs taste best when harvested ripe, and only last about three days as a fresh fruit. Pick figs when they are somewhat soft to the touch, chill if preferred and eat within a few days. Cultivars that dry well should be dried directly upon picking.

Along with eating figs fresh or dried, you can bake with figs. Fig bars taste great, or, instead of applesauce, fig puree can be used to replace oils used in baked cookies and cakes. This will naturally help hold in the moisture, keeping baked goods fresher longer.

JUJUBE *(Ziziphus jujuba)*

Jujube is a graceful landscape tree that requires little attention to provide fruit.

One excellent way to save home energy costs is to grow a tree that shades your home in summer then drops its leaves and lets the sun warm your home in winter. If you can eat the fruit of the tree, well, what a wonderful added bonus! Next add to the fact that the tree survives 120°F and down to minus 20°F and is a lovely, upright shade tree with bright green leaves. The quick-growing tree reaches 15 to 30 feet tall, and 10 to 20 feet wide with branches growing in a zig-zag pattern. The wood is very hard and strong. Plants tend to be thorny, but this is highly variable. Thorniness is not an issue since fruit is easily harvested by allowing it to drop. Fruit is the size of a cherry or slightly larger, and some say the taste and consistency is like that of a date or an apple. Fruit is reddish to brown when ripe, its smooth skin wrinkling like a date as it dries. Like a date each fruit has a single pit inside.

Flowers are fragrant but small, about ¼ inch across, and white or greenish-yellow. Pollination needs of the jujube are not clearly defined, but appears to be done by ants or other insects and possibly by the wind. Most jujube cultivars produce fruit without cross-pollination. Jujube fruiting is well protected from late frosts by flowering only after all chance of cold weather has passed.

■ *Recommended Varieties*

'GA-866' has larger fruit and is good for Upper Desert Zone. 'Lang' is almost spineless and dries well. 'Li' is nearly thornless and needs a second plant as pollinator. 'Sherwood' is best for Desert Zones and can self-pollinate. 'So' is a more dwarf form, good for small spaces. 'Sugar Cane' is spiny but sweetest of all and needs to cross pollinate with 'So', 'Li', or 'Lang.'

Pollination: Self-fertile but yields are better with cross-pollination, even with another plant of the same variety.

Chill Hours: Jujube requires 100 to 150 chill hours.

Planting

Jujubes should be given a warm, sunny location, but are otherwise relatively undemanding. Given adequate heat and sun, the trees will thrive without any special care. Another excellent tree for the beginner, or for an aging gardener who wants less to maintain.

Soils: Jujubes tolerate many types of soils, soils with high salinity or high alkalinity, but prefer a sandy, well-drained soil over heavy, poorly drained soil.

Maintenance

Water: One of the outstanding qualities of the jujube tree is its tolerance of drought conditions. Regular watering, though, is important to ensure a quality fruit crop, generally 20 inches of water per year in nondormant months. Like all trees, water should be applied so that it reaches the 3-foot depth.

Fertilization: Fertilizer requirements have not been studied, but jujubes appear to do well with little or no fertilization. Light broadcast applications of a balanced fertilizer at two-month intervals during the growing season will speed growth. Do not fertilize until the newly planted tree has several months to get established.

Pruning: Unpruned trees produce as well as trees that have been pruned. If you chose to prune, do so in winter when plants are dormant.

Pests: There are no known pests in the Southwest.

Harvest & Storage

Fruit ripens in late summer into fall. The freshly harvested fruits as well as the candied dried fruits are eaten as a snack, and the fruits can also be made into jelly or even wine. The crop ripens non-simultaneously, and fruit can be picked for three to six weeks from a single tree. If picked green, jujubes will not ripen. Ripe fruits may be stored at room temperature for about a week. Dried fruit stores indefinitely, especially if it dried on the tree. In some countries jujube fruit are deseeded and preserved in hard liquor (vodka or rum) then eaten on special occasions.

MESQUITE *(Prosopis* species)

One very popular tree in our Southwestern landscapes is the mesquite tree. And most mesquite have edible seed pods, but sweetest of all is the native velvet mesquite (*Prosopis velutina*), seconded by the honey mesquite (*Prosopis glandulosa*). Locally, mesquite is dubbed the "Candy Bar Tree." You can chew on fresh, ripe sweet mesquite pods straight from the tree. Look for those with red stripes on the pods, the redder the better (sweeter). The edible pods of mesquite can be as sweet tasting as a candy bar, but far better than candy bars; the pods are a "slow-release" food. This means that although they taste sweet, they have a low glycemic index. They are filled with soluble fibers that keep your blood sugar from spiking. A safe candy bar tree! The thick, non-native mesquite pods from South America are often bitter. Test pods before you collect tons of them.

■ *Recommended Varieties*

Velvet mesquite (*Prosopis velutina*) and honey mesquite (*Prosopis glandulosa*) are preferred.

Pollination: Mesquite is widely said to be wind pollinated, but have you ever tasted mesquite honey? The flowers are a spectacular nectar source for bees. Once all spent blooms drop, I rake all the tiny petals up for the compost bin.

Chill Hours: 200 to 300 hours.

■ *Planting*

Mesquite can be planted from nursery stock, but take care to avoid damaging the taproot. Alternatively, find a tree with tasty pods and harvest a handful of seed pods. Plant them, pods and all, where you want your tree to grow. Water and stand back. When about twenty little seedlings have clusters of true leaves, select the one that looks best and remove the rest. Keep watering but do not fertilize. Our tree grown this way reached 20 feet in three years. Since all mesquites can cross, it is now hard to find pure velvet mesquite. The Desert Legume Program, a nonprofit group in Tucson, Arizona, will send a few seeds to interested growers.

■ *Maintenance*

Water: Mesquite does best with 20 inches of water per year. Since they are semi-dormant in winter, the time to water

them is spring and summer. Water wide and water deep. Apply the water out at the dripline and be sure it goes 3 feet deep. If you plant from seed, weekly watering gets the tree growing fast. A mature, established tree can use water once a month in summer.

Fertilizer: Do not fertilize any member of the legume family.

Pruning: Resist the urge to try to turn this tree into a lollipop! Mesquite grow tall, but with arching branches that shade the soil and their trunks from searing sun. Work with this form and prune as necessary to keep branches out of harm's way.

Pests: None noted.

Harvest your mesquite pods from the tree.

■ *Harvest & Storage*

To make mesquite meal or flour you will need to harvest pods directly from the tree. Ones that have hit the ground may pick up soil-borne *Aspergillus* fungal spores which produce aflatoxin, and are not killed by processing. Rinse your pods and toast them. Bake whole at 200°F for two to three hours, until they are a toasty tan color. Stir them every so often to prevent burning. Once toasted, grind pods in a blender. Process only a handful at a time, for 20 to 30 seconds. Grind for less time and you get a mesquite meal, which can be used instead of cornmeal in any recipe. Pour the result through a sifter and collect the flour. If you have a coffee or hand mill, those work well, too. If you don't toast them first, you may not be able to grind them.

You can get too much of a good thing. The high levels of soluble fibers may cause intestinal discomfort for some people. Eat moderate amounts until your body has become accustomed to these foods. Mesquite pods, and their meal and flour, are considered a slow-release food due to galactomannan gums which have been found to lower glycemic responses. Their glycemic index is 25 percent, compared to 60 for sweet corn, and 100 for white sugar.

OLIVE *(Olea europaea)*

Harvest olives when the skin is still firm.

Olives are grown for their fruit, which is used either for oil or cured for eating. Oil olives can also be cured for eating, but their flesh is considered inferior in flavor and texture. Most home gardeners prefer an eating (table) olive or a dual-purpose tree. For table olives, you need to select from those you cure when green or those cured when ripe (purple to black).

Olive plants are lovely evergreens with narrow silvery leaves and decorative gnarled trunks. Olives are more shrubby in nature than stately trees, because they need shade for the lower trunk, especially on the south side of the plant. Trees that get sun on their trunks will grow a profuse amount of suckers or watersprouts out of the base to provide shade for themselves. Plan accordingly when you decide where to put your olive tree. A shading structure or shrubs will permit you to have the trunk showing. Olives grow well in partial shade, which means you can grow them in containers. Bring them indoors in the upper zones. Olive trees can last for a millennium. The oldest proven ones are in the Galilee region and are over 3,000 years old.

■ *Recommended Varieties*

Middle and Upper Desert: 'Arbequina', oil and table olive, self-fertile, good in containers in upper elevations.

Low and Middle Desert: 'Ascolana' green table olive, better if crossed; 'Kalamata', table and oil olive, better if crossed, good in containers in upper elevations; 'Sevillano', table olive, better if crossed.

Middle Desert: 'Chemlali', oil and table olive, self-fertile; 'Frantoio', table and oil olive, better if crossed, good in containers in upper elevations.

Middle and Upper Desert: 'Manzanillo', table olive, self-fertile, good frost resistance, good in containers in upper elevations.

Low, Middle, and Upper Desert: 'Mission', table olive, self-fertile, good in containers in upper elevations; 'Queen', green table olive, better if crossed, good in containers in upper elevations.

Pollination: Most will self-pollinate, but two different varieties will help ensure good fruit set.

Chill Hours: 200 to 300 for best fruit set.

■ *Planting*

Olives are best planted in autumn, as they are genetically programmed to respond to the winter rains that occur in the Mediterranean.

Soil: Here is the reason for including olives—they have a marked preference for alkaline soils! They grow in virtually any soil as long as it does not stay cold and soggy. In rich soils they are predisposed to disease and produce less well than in poorer soil.

■ *Maintenance*

Water: 15 to 20 inches of water per year, applied in the warm months. Roots need to dry between watering.

Fertilizer: No fertilizer is required.

Pruning: Olives flower on second year wood, which may tempt you to never prune them, but you do need to remove old wood and encourage new fruiting wood to grow. Also, reduce pest problems by allowing some light and air into the center of the tree. Prune in early spring before the olive starts to flower, every one to three years. Cut off any crossing branches and thin out some of the remaining branches to allow light in.

Pests: Pests on home trees are rare indeed. If you happen to be near a commercial grove you may get the olive fruit fly which lays its eggs in the olive fruit before it becomes ripe in the autumn, rendering them bitter and inedible. Kaolin spray will kill the pest. Black scale may also appear, a small black insect that resembles a small black spot. They attach themselves firmly to olive trees and reduce the quality of the fruit; their main predators are wasps. Common scale can be a problem on container plants indoors. Bring them outdoors where predators can eat these pests. Rabbits, javalina, and deer can eat the bark of olive trees and can do considerable damage, especially to young trees. Protect against these herbivores.

■ *Harvest & Storage*

Ask around in your community. Sometimes people share an olive oil press. Otherwise you will need to cure your olives either green or ripe. This can be done with brine (dissolved salt), dry salt, or a lye solution. There are any number of recipes on the web or available from your Cooperative Extension Service.

Pecan trees are large, full-sized landscape trees.

PECAN *(Carya illinoinensis)*

Despite having "Illinois" in the scientific name, pecans can be grown in much of the Southwest. This is because there are two "land races" of pecans, and their origins go back to the last Ice Age. Southern pecans got pushed south by the glaciers, while the Northern pecans hung out on the edge of the glaciers. You can fill in the blanks! Middle and High Desert will need to plant Southern pecans, while Cool Highlands plant the Northern pecans.

Pecan trees are large at maturity, 40 to 50 feet, and large in diameter, too. Before you dig your planting hole, look out and up and check any views you might have, plus avoid planting under power lines. Plant pecan trees 30 to 40 feet apart. Pecan trees may live and bear edible seeds for more than 300 years, a lasting legacy indeed.

■ Recommended Varieties

Pecans require cross-pollination from another variety of pecan. The number of varieties and the relationships between them is a worthy topic for a doctoral thesis (it's been done) but beyond the scope of this book. Ideally, discuss the selections with your local County Cooperative Extension Agent before ordering plants. That said, here are some broad recommendations.

If you can only have one pecan tree, 'Western Schley' is recommended; it is often self-fertile, although an additional tree of another variety will improve fruit set.

Middle Desert: select from 'Apache', 'Burkett', 'Cheyenne', 'Choctaw', 'Mohawk', 'Western Schley', or 'Wichita'.
High Desert: select from 'Apache', 'Cherokee', 'Cheyenne', 'Choctaw', 'Mohawk', or 'Pawnee', or 'Western Schley'.
Cool Highlands: select from 'Desirable', 'Kanza', 'Northern', 'Pawnee', or 'Western Schley'.

Pollination: Cross-pollination is required.
Chill Hours: 400 to 600 hours required. Varies with variety. Plant as recommended for your area.

■ Planting

Avoid a container-grown tree that is larger than 5 or 6 feet tall. Pecans have taproots and this makes them hard to transplant. Bare-root pecan trees should be avoided in the arid Southwest.

Soil: Pecans require well-drained soil and can tolerate rocks, and even clay, but if you have a thick caliche layer in your yard, break through it beneath the tree before you plant, otherwise the roots will drown in the caliche bathtub.

■ *Maintenance*

Water: Trees grow and produce best with 30 to 40 inches of water during the growing season. Water is especially important once plants have bloomed and nuts are forming.

Fertilizer: Pecan trees are susceptible to nutrient problems, especially low zinc and magnesium. Watch for these deficiency problems and nip them in the bud by mulching the trees well out to the drip line of the leaves with compost and watering through this compost layer to get the minerals into the soil. Many people also use a light dose of dissolved Epsom salts (magnesium sulfate) to deliver magnesium to the tree. A fertilizer with ample phosphorous is also required for best fruit production. Yearly application of rock phosphate is a good solution to this issue.

Pests: Once they figure out how tasty the nuts are, any wildlife will go for them. Climbing pests like squirrels and pack rats will climb the trees. Wrap the trunk with a metal shield, 5 feet off the ground. You can attach the shield with spikes that you withdraw slightly each year as the tree grows.

Pecan scab is a major disease problem for pecans. Clean up fallen leaves, twigs, and nuts from the previous year and throw them away or give them to a friend who doesn't grow pecans for composting.

■ *Harvest & Storage*

Harvest nuts once they start to drop. You can lay sheets or tarps under the trees and shake the branches to loosen the nuts. Once harvested, cure the nuts to avoid mold problems, even in our arid area. Lay nuts in a single layer in a warm, dry place. If space is an issue, cure in shallow cardboard boxes, like those that soda cans come in, or nursery plant flats, which can be stacked with air spaces between them. Remove the husks and give to a friend who doesn't have pecan trees for compost. Use the nuts within three months for best flavor. You can also freeze nuts in plastic bags until you're ready to use them.

PINEAPPLE GUAVA
(*Acca sellowiana,* formerly *Feijoa sellowiana*)

Pineapple guava is not the same as the true guava used in Hawaiian Punch fruit drink, although both are in the same plant family. Their family includes a number of tropical and subtropical plants, including cloves, eucalyptus, and myrtle. I tell you this to introduce you to a unique plant family with some members that will thrive in the Southwest. Pineapple guava is one that will grow well in all but the Cool Highlands and Cold Mountains, where it will have to be grown in containers.

Pineapple guava is a charming, drought-tolerant evergreen shrub with blue-green leaves the size of silver dollars. You can plant a hedge to form a dense, screening 8- to 15-foot-tall barrier between you and a noisy street. Even better, this attractive plant grows and fruits in partial shade, thus you can plant it on the shady north side of the home, or grow it in the reduced light situations found inside your home. In containers, pineapple guavas can be trained into compact 4- to 7-foot plants. The delicate white with purple flowers appear on new wood, so excessive pruning will deny you the taste of the plum-sized fruit. It has a unique, sort of a pineapple flavor with a taste of spearmint.

◼ *Recommended Varieties*

Low Desert: 'Apollo', 'Coolidge', 'Pineapple Gem'.

Middle Desert: 'Apollo', 'Coolidge', 'Mammoth', 'Pineapple Gem'.

High Desert: 'Mammoth', 'Nazemetz', 'Nikita', 'Pineapple Gem', and 'Robert' (self-fertile but requires two plants).

Cool Highlands and Cold Mountains: The above varieties can all be grown in containers; however, due to length of season, consider 'Mammoth', 'Nazemetz', or 'Nikita.'

Pollination: Bees do the work and most varieties are self-pollinating, but mix varieties for best fruit set.

Chill Hours: 50 hours minimum, 100 to 200 preferred for best fruit production.

◼ *Planting*

Soil: Well-drained soil is required. Add ample compost prior to planting and mulch beneath the plant with its fallen leaves to help retain moisture and recycle nutrients.

■ *Maintenance*

Water: No clear guidelines are established, but an estimated 20 to 30 inches of water per year will be more than enough, less for shade-grown plants.

Fertilizer: For optimal fruit set, a bloom fertilizer applied when flowers are evident is good. Shrubs do well with mulched roots and a general purpose fertilizer monthly during the warm season.

Pruning: If you wish a dense shrub, prune dominant vertical branches frequently when young to encourage a full, dense form. Flowers appear on new wood, so once the plant has attained its ideal size for your yard, prune back roughly 6 inches all over once per year after you harvest the fruit. Avoid summer pruning.

Pests: No known pests.

■ *Harvest & Storage*

Fruit ripens four to seven months after flowering depending on variety and location—usually between September and January. The leather grayish green skin of the fully ripened fruit blends in with the foliage, except for some varieties that turn purplish on the side exposed to the sun. Fruit can be picked before it ripens and allowed to ripen at room temperature. Or if you get it the day it falls, it has perfect ripeness.

You have to hunt for the fruit, but it is worth it!

Depending on variety, fruit can be from ¾ to 4 inches in size. Cut them open to reveal the amber to pale green flesh that is juicy, tasty, and wonderfully fragrant. You may also see numerous black seeds that are edible and much like that of a kiwi. If you grew a landscape plant as opposed to a fruiting variety, the seeds may be large and less palatable.

Some people eat them skin and all, others prefer to eat only the softer inner portion. They can also be made into jelly, jam, and juice.

Flower petals are edible and quite tasty in salads, with a mild cinnamon taste.

For the best fruit set, plant more than one pomegranate tree.

POMEGRANATE
(Punica granatum)

Autumn is for apples in some parts of the world, but in desert climes, autumn is for pomegranates. Literally a "fruit of grains," open one of these leathery skinned fruits, and you can easily see where the name comes from. The fruit is filled with a hundred or so small seeds, each seed covered with a fleshy coating. Use your tongue to crush the flesh-covered seed against the roof of your mouth. Savor the burst of sweet/tart juice. The tiny white seeds themselves are somewhat bitter, and traditionally you spit them out. But not at your little sister. Or not more than once anyway.

Likewise, you could simply enjoy this drought-tolerant shrub for its shiny green leaves, carnation-like crimson flowers in spring, glowing globes of scarlet in early autumn, followed by gloriously golden-yellow autumn color to the leaves, just before they drop to reveal the pale gray bark with patches of sienna color. Birds like to nest in the boughs of this large shrub, which can be pruned into a small tree shape. Plants reach 12 to 15 feet tall. You can plant a mass of them closely together to form a privacy screen, or grow a dwarf variety in a large container.

Enjoy having a bit of history in your yard as well. Mention of pomegranates is made in the Bible, the Koran, as well as in ancient Greek, Roman, Persian, Indian, and Chinese tales. Pomegranates were cultivated and featured in artwork of ancient Egypt and Mesopotamia, as well as on the scepter of King Solomon.

■ Recommended Varieties

There are tall tree-like cultivars, shrubby ones, and dwarf cultivars to grow in containers. Buy locally grown plants whenever possible to increase the chance of survival, and avoid plants bred in humid Florida. In these varieties, fruit and then flesh color is noted in parentheses.

Low Desert: 'Crab' (red, red), 'Home' (yellow, pink), 'Kino Heritage' (pale red, red), 'Kino Heritage White' (greenish, white), 'Sweet' (greenish, pink).

Middle Desert: 'Balegal' (pink, red), 'Early Wonderful ' (red, red), 'Green Globe' (green, pink), 'Kino Heritage' (pale red, red), 'Kino Heritage White' (greenish, white), 'Sweet' (greenish, pink).

Upper Desert: 'Cloud' (green-red, white), 'Early Wonderful ' (red, red), 'Green Globe' (green, pink), 'Kino Heritage' (pale red, red), 'Kino Heritage White' (greenish, white), 'Utah Sweet' (pink, pink).

Pollination: While cross-pollination is not required, planting at least two plants, even if the same variety, improves the chance of fruit set.

Chill Hours: 100 to 200.

■ Planting

Plant pomegranates in the fall or spring. If you live in the cooler regions of the Southwest, plant in a sheltered location to prevent cold damage which will occur much below 10°F.

Soil: Soil must be well-drained, and while loamy soil is preferred, average Southwest soil without caliche is acceptable.

■ *Maintenance*

Water: Water to establish the plants, then be sure the plants get 20 inches of water per year, especially during the hot summer months.

Fertilizer: Form tree wells around your plants and add ample compost every spring for best fruit set. Otherwise, fertilize three times a year with a well-balanced fertilizer.

Pests and Diseases: Pomegranates are relatively free of most pests and diseases. Unlike many fruit trees you can (and should) leave the fallen leaves under the trees to help mulch them for winter.

■ *Harvest & Storage*

Depending on variety, pomegranates are ready to harvest from August through October. Since there are a number of white varieties, color is not a reliable indicator, nor is waiting for fruit to drop because the ripe fruit can hang onto the tree for months. The fruits are ripe when they have developed their distinctive color and make a metallic sound when tapped. The fruits must be picked before overly ripe or they tend to crack open. Once harvested, they can be kept up to six months in the refrigerator without shrinking or spoiling.

To easily open a pomegranate without stain or bowls of water, try this. Score the rind around the "waist" without cutting deeply into the fruit. Grasp firmly and twist the two halves apart. Hold the open end over a bowl and give the rind a series of hard whacks with a sturdy wooden spoon. The juicy seeds will just fall out intact.

Pomegranate juice tastes just plain glorious, and it is filled with all sorts of healthy, nutritious compounds our bodies need. To make juice, use a citrus juicer and set it to as little pulp as possible. The seeds inside the flesh juicy part can impart a bitter flavor. Consume juice raw or cook the juice with sugar and pectin to create a tasty, claret-colored jelly. Cook with sugar alone to create grenadine, a nice addition to your cocktail cabinet.

You can also enjoy pomegranate by rolling an intact one on a hard surface, pushing down hard and crushing all the juicy bits inside. Use an ice pick or narrow knife to make a hole just big enough for a drinking straw, insert, and sip away. Voilá! The original "box" of juice, 100 percent natural, wonderfully biodegradable, and entirely "green."

Pomegranates grow best in the warmer areas of the Southwest.

POME FRUITS

With the right selection of variety, apples and other pome fruits can be grown in the cooler areas of the Southwest.

If you have ever cut an apple in two through the "waist" you may have noticed how the seeds form a star shape in the center. This star shape helps define the pome fruits, which are all in the Rose family. A number of pome fruits can be grown in the Southwest, and here I include some of the more popular ones.

Years ago, I stopped at a roadside stand in New Mexico, tempted by the apples on display. The farmer asked me if I had ever heard of Washington apples. Sure. The upshot of the tale is that New Mexico lets Washington brag all they want because in the Land of Enchantment they know their own apples are the finest. I am inclined to agree. Something about the warm sunny days and clear cool nights makes for wonderfully crisp and flavorful fruit.

Apples and pears are eaten raw or cooked, while mountain ash (also called rowan) and quince are cooked prior to use. All of these fruits can easily and successfully be grown in the High Desert and Cool Highlands zones; indeed, many commercial orchards are located in these areas. Due to chill hour requirements, you can also grow these in the Middle Desert but the varieties to select from are more limited. Low Desert will have a very hard time meeting the chill needs for pome fruit. In the Cold Mountains, you can grow these but prepare yourself for disappointment every few years when a late freeze kills the blooms before they turn into fruit.

■ Recommended Varieties

Cross-pollination is required with all of these, thus you must plant (at least) two of each type of fruit, the few exceptions are noted. All have required chill hours. The varieties recommended for each zone have the appropriate chill hours and heat tolerance.

APPLES (*Malus domesticus*): (Chill hours 400 to 1500)
Cold Mountains: 'Arkansas Black', 'Braeburn', 'Golden Delicious', 'Red Delicious'.
Cool Highlands: 'Arkansas Black', 'Braeburn', 'Empire', 'Firm Gold', 'Fuji', 'Golden Delicious', 'Granny Smith', 'Gravenstein', 'Lodi', 'Red Delicious', 'Summered'.
High Desert: 'Braeburn', 'Dorsett', 'Firm Gold', 'Fuji'.
Middle Desert: 'Anna', 'Beverly Hills', 'Dorset', 'Ein Shemer'.
Low Desert: 'Beverly Hills', 'Ein Shemer'.

MOUNTAIN ASH (*Sorbus* species): (Chill hours 300 to 800)
These trees can be grown in partial shade and will do better with afternoon shade at the lower elevations.
Cold Mountains: 'Ivan's Beauty', 'Rabinia', 'Rosina', 'Shipova'.
Cool Highlands: 'Ivan's Beauty', 'Rabinia', 'Rosina', 'Shipova'.
High Desert: 'Ivan's Beauty', 'Rabinia', 'Rosina'.
Middle Desert: 'Rabinia', 'Rosina'.

QUINCE, FLOWERING (*Chaenomeles* species): (Chill hours 500 to 1000)
Cold Mountains: 'Contorted', 'Tanechka', 'Toyo-Nishiki'.
Cool Highlands: 'Contorted', 'Tanechka', 'Toyo-Nishiki', 'Victory'.
High Desert: 'Victory'.

QUINCE, FRUITING (*Cydonia oblonga*): (Chill hours 100 to 450)
Cold Mountains: 'Orange', 'Pineapple', 'Smyrna', 'Wonderful'.
Cool Highlands: 'Orange', 'Pineapple', 'Smyrna', 'Wonderful'.
High Desert: 'Kino Heritage', 'Orange', 'Pineapple', 'Smyrna'.
Middle Desert: 'Kino Heritage', 'Orange', 'Pineapple', 'Smyrna'.
Low Desert: 'Champion', 'Kino Heritage'.

PEAR (*Pyrus* species): (Chill hours 400 to 1500)
Cold Mountains: 'Bartlett', 'Bosc', 'Hood', 'Red Sensation', '20th Century Asian'.
Cool Highlands: 'Bartlett', 'Bosc', 'Florida Home', 'Hood', 'Red Sensation', 'Seckel', '20th Century Asian'.
High Desert: 'Florida Home', 'Seckel', 'Surecrop', '20th Century Asian', 'Yakumo Asian'.
Middle Desert: 'Keiffer', 'LeConte', 'Seckel', 'Shinseiki Asian', 'Surecrop', 'Yakumo Asian'.
Low Desert: 'Keiffer', 'LeConte', 'Shinseiki Asian'.

◼ *Planting*

All of these pome fruits should be planted in early spring from container plants. Bare-root trees have a poor success rate in our arid environment. In the Desert zones, consider planting in early autumn if you can find the plants then.

Soil: Loamy, well-drained soil with a pH of 6.5 to 7.2 is best. Fruiting quince will tolerate soils to pH 7.8.

◼ *Maintenance*

Water: Quince are quite drought tolerant, requiring 20 to 30 inches of water per year. The rest of these trees with northern genes will require ample moisture for good fruit production, 50 to 80 inches per year depending on size and location. Apply on a regular basis. In the Desert zones, water once a month in winter if we don't get substantial rain. Apply a thick layer of cedar bark mulch to help reduce evaporation and protect roots of these trees from sunbaking, and help those in higher elevations to survive winter cold better. Keep mulch 3 inches away from the trunk to avoid disease issues.

Fertilizer: Apply fertilizer once per month when leaves are present. Use a fruiting fertilizer once the trees begin to bloom, and through harvest.

Pruning: All of these can be trained into their mature form when young. Watch the trees with heavy fruit carefully as the fruit ripens. If there is too much for a single limb, you will have to remove some fruit or the entire branch may break off.

Pests: Apple maggot, plum curculio, and codling moth are the "big three" pests of stone and pome fruits in the Southwest. These insects appear with the blooms and are all best treated with biological controls. Fireblight (caused by a wind-borne bacteria) can appear at any time and is a problem in the Southwest for these woody members of the Rose family. Fireblight shows itself, seemingly overnight, as brown, dried-up leaves on specific branches. Remove and discard diseased tissue immediately, including any fallen leaves. It's difficult to control this disease, and entire plants may have to be removed from your garden if it spreads.

■ *Harvest & Storage*

Enjoy apples fresh, baked, processed into preserves, or cubed and frozen for future baking.

Mountain ash fruit is made into syrup, cordials, and preserves. It is also highly attractive to birds and is a good food source for them in midwinter. Consider leaving some fruits on the tree to share.

Quince are rock hard at maturity and ready to harvest 100 to 140 days after flowering, depending on the variety. Quince are generally cooked into preserves or the popular paste called *dulce de membrillo*, and they also make a dandy cordial.

Pears vary and some are only good for cooking, like the Kieffer, but others are best fresh off the tree. Pear can also be made into preserves and cordials.

Bosc pears ready for picking.

STONE FRUITS

All these species of *Prunus* are deciduous trees that are generally short-lived, bearing fruit within three to four years of being planted and living out their life within thirty years. Not just short lived, but short in stature as well, which makes them nice for smaller yards. Even if you never get much fruit, the spring blooms are beautiful, so you could plant them as ornamentals in the landscape.

What is an almond doing in with all these fruit? Almonds are kissing cousins to the rest of these fruit, and have been bred for the yummy seed inside. Once you grow them you will realize they are just like a peach that never gets fleshy.

■ *Recommended Varieties*

Cross pollination is required with almost all of these, thus you must plant at least two varieties of each type of fruit. (If they can self-pollinate, it is noted) All require chill hours. Varieties are recommended by zone with appropriate chill hours for that zone. Note that the issue with trying to grow some of these fruits is not the chill hours but the sheer heat of summer.

Almonds ready for the harvest.

ALMOND (*Prunus amygdalus*): (Chill hours 200 to 600)
High Desert: 'All-in-One' (self), 'Garden Prince' (self).
Middle Desert: 'All-in-One' (self), 'Garden Prince' (self),
'Mission', 'Neplus Ultra', 'Nonpareil', 'Peerless', 'Price',
'Texas Mission'.

APRICOT (*Prunus* species): (Chill hours 400 to 1,000)
Cold Mountains: 'Chinese', 'Gold Cot', 'Mormon', 'Tilton'.
Cool Highlands: 'Gold Kist', 'Gold Cot', 'Goldrich', 'Modesto',
'Moorpark', 'Patterson', 'Royal Rosa', 'Royal' (Blenheim),
'Tilton', 'Wenatchee'.
High Desert: 'Gold Kist', 'Gold Cot', 'Goldrich', 'Katy', 'Royal'
(Blenheim), 'Wenatchee'.
Middle Desert: 'Gold Kist', 'Golden Amber', 'Katy', 'Royal'
(Blenheim).
Low Desert: 'Katy'.

CHERRY (*Prunus* species): (Chill hours 600 to 1,200)
Cold Mountains: Only sour (cooking) cherries can be grown in
this zone, select from 'Montmorency' or 'North Star'.
Cool Highlands: The sour cherries mentioned above can be
grown in this zone as well as the following sweet cherries:
'Bing', 'Lambert', 'Rainier', 'Stella', 'Van'.

NECTARINE (*Prunus persica*): (Chill hours 650 to 850)
Cool Highlands: 'Fantasia', 'Firebright', 'Flavortop', 'Redgold',
'Sun Glo', 'Sun Grand'.
High Desert: '2W68W'.
Middle Desert: 'Armking', 'Desert Dawn'.

PEACH (*Prunus persica*): (Chill hours 400 to 900)
Peaches are popular and there are myriad varieties to select
from. Here are some proven performers for each zone.

Cold Mountains: 'Fairhaven', 'Halehaven', 'Halford', 'Indian Blood
Cling', 'Madison', 'Polly', 'Reliance', 'Veteran'.
Cool Highlands: 'Belle of Georgia', 'Cresthaven', 'Fay Elberta',
'Redskin', 'Rio Oso Gem', 'Sunhaven', 'White Heath Cling'.
High Desert: 'August Pride', 'Babcock', 'Desert Gold', 'Rio Oso
Gem', 'Sweet Ventura'.
Middle Desert: 'August Pride', 'Babcock', 'Desert Gold',
'Midpride', 'Sweet Ventura', 'Tropical Snow'.
Low Desert: 'August Pride', 'Desert Gold', 'Flordagrande',
'Flordaking', 'Flordaprince', 'Midpride', 'Tropic Snow'.

Ripe fruits of a Stanley plum tree.

PLUM (*Prunus* species): (Chill hours 100 to 1,200)
Plums come in three main genetic groups, Japanese, European, and North American. The ones listed here for most of the zones are those that will self-pollinate. If you have the space and taste for plums, there are many others you can select from.

Cold Mountains (these will need a pollinizer): 'Ember', 'Ozark Premier', 'Pipestone'.
Cool Highlands: 'Methley', 'Satsuma', 'Stanley', 'Sugar'.
High Desert: *Prunus mexicana* or these cultivars: 'Satsuma', 'Stanley'.
Middle Desert: *Prunus mexicana* or these cultivars: 'Satsuma', 'Stanley'.
Low Desert: *Prunus mexicana*.

■ *Planting*

All of these stone fruits should be planted in early spring, from container plants. Bare root trees have a poor success rate in our arid environment. In the Desert zones, consider planting in early autumn if you can find the plants then.

Soil: Loamy, well-drained soil with a pH of 6.5 to 7.2 is best. Almond and Mexican plum will tolerate soils to pH 7.5.

■ *Maintenance*

Water: These small trees with northern genes will require ample moisture for good fruit production, 40 to 50 inches per year depending on size and location. Apply on a regular basis. In the Desert zones, water once a month in winter if we don't get substantial rain. Apply a thick layer of cedar bark mulch to help reduce evaporation and protect roots of these trees from sunbaking, and help those in higher elevations to survive winter cold better. Keep mulch 3 inches away from the trunk to avoid disease issues.

Fertilizer: Apply fertilizer once per month when leaves are present. Use a fruiting fertilizer once the trees begin to bloom, and through harvest.

Pruning: Peaches and some species of cherry can become large trees. All of these can be trained into their mature form when young. The only mature pruning they may need is to remove dead wood.

The exception is the trees with heavy fruit—watch them carefully as the fruit ripens. If there is too much weight for a single limb, you will have to remove some fruit or the entire branch may break off.

Pests: Apple maggot, plum curculio, and codling moth constitute the "big three" pests of stone and pome fruits in the Southwest. These insects appear with the blooms and are all best treated with biological controls. Fireblight (caused by a wind-borne bacteria) can appear at any time and is a problem in the Southwest for these woody members of the rose family. Fireblight shows itself, seemingly overnight, as brown, dried-up leaves on specific branches. Remove diseased tissue, including any fallen leaves and throw it in the trash immediately. It's difficult to control this disease, and entire plants may have to be removed from your garden if it spreads.

■ *Harvest & Storage*

Almonds should be harvested and cured just as is done for pecans. Eat apricots fresh, process into preserves, or dry into fruit leather, or cubed and frozen. Enjoy cherries fresh, baked, or processed into preserves. They can also be pitted and frozen.

Nectarines can be eaten fresh, processed into preserves, or cubed and frozen. Enjoy peaches fresh, baked, processed into preserves, or cubed and frozen. Eat plums fresh, processed into preserves or dried into fruit leather. I also cube and freeze them for plum pudding at Winter Solstice.

CHAPTER 7

VEGETABLE & HERB GARDENING

Fruits and vegetables all taste much better when freshly picked and eaten. Tomatoes, corn, oranges, or kale—food right out of the garden is fresh and vital, in the sense of being filled with life (from *vita*, Latin for life). Store-bought produce may have been picked one month to one *year* prior to being sold. No matter how good the storage techniques, once severed from the plant, the tissue begins to die, and the flavor and nutrients degenerate.

Vegetable Gardening Throughout the Year

Earlier in the book I mentioned that in parts of the Southwest you can have five different gardens per year. Since the Southwest includes areas more like Canada in climate, this has been simplified to two seasons, cool and warm. Since plants are genetically programmed to grow best in specific conditions, you will need to plan and plant the right crop at the right time of year. In the Cold Mountains, your main garden season is summer, and you can have broccoli rubbing shoulders with peppers—not the case in the Low Desert!

Books written "Back East" always talk as if the garden year begins in spring, but autumn planting makes sense in most of our area. Why not enjoy the use of your land right through the winter? Even if you live in the Cold Mountains, think how wonderful it is to go out in the dead of winter and dig some parsnips out from under their snow over—their sweetness is fully developed!

Growing herbs in a small kitchen garden or in containers by the back door makes it more likely that you'll use them.

Garden Seasons in the Southwest

REGION	Jan.	Feb.	March	April	May	June	July	Aug.	Sept.	Oct.	Nov.	Dec.
Cold Mountains												
Cool Highlands												
High Desert												
Middle Desert												
Low Desert												

KEY: ☐ None ■ Cool Season ☐ Warm Season ■ Cold/Warm Season* ☐ Warm/Cold Season*
*Cusp months (transition your garden between the seasons)

For those of you who prefer words to charts, here are two simple tips for planting at the correct time:

- Warm-season vegetables can be planted after danger of frost, and when soil temperature is above 60°F. These vegetables are mostly the ones that flower and bear fruit (like corn and zucchini).
- Cool-season vegetables don't much like the heat of summer. In our area this means plant in fall and again in spring (or vice versa).

The vegetable and herb profiles are organized to help you distinguish cool- and warm-season plants so there is no question as to which to plant when.

Transitioning between Cool- and Warm-Season Gardening

The hardest part of gardening is pulling up one crop to make space for another. You may have to be ruthless if you want to enjoy an orderly succession of garden produce, or for organized folks, carefully plan. A bit of planning is the better choice, ounce of prevention and all that.

If you have rented a backhoe and replaced a section of your Southwestern soil with good garden soil, then you are lucky, and you can plant your garden in rows and blocks and easily transition through the seasons. Since many of us have raised beds to avoid dealing with harsh Southwestern soils (and stooping over), transitioning from season to season becomes more of a challenge. You may have to be creative and consider pots as holding areas for plants to reside in for a while until you can put them into the garden. This may lead to an array of large pots as container gardens, and before you know it you will get more pots as holding areas, and so on!

No matter how your garden grows, a little bit of planning goes a long way when making the transition. Sit down with your wish list of plants, grid paper, and colored pencils, markers, or my choice—highlighters. You could mark each plant on your wish list with a color to match the month it has to go into the garden. If your entire list is in one month, will it all fit? Instead expand your choices and your seasons.

Draw your garden space on the grid paper. Note where north is, because taller plants will need to go on that end so as to not shade shorter ones (only where appropriate—in Low Desert you may want to shade some). Now start playing with the colors. Warm-season corn (pink marker) can go in the same space as the cool-season radish (blue marker). Warm cucumbers can follow cool arugula. When this plan comes to the real world, you can pull all but a few arugula (leave them widely spaced) and plant your cucumbers between them. Once the cucumbers are large enough to need the space the arugula will be flowered and gone.

One excellent reason for all this planning is so that when you go shopping, you will not be tempted to get a few extra plants. Crowded plants do not grow well, and you will have wasted your money. Also, save these maps from year to year because some crops should not be planted in the same space the following year, and a record of what you did is useful.

Find Your Favorites

Ready to plan your planting? Here is a mini-index to the vegetables and herbs discussed in this chapter. Some of them are combined with plants that have similar habits and needs, like broccoli combined with cauliflower.

Plant just a few radish seeds at a time, over a period of several weeks to enjoy a continuous harvest.

Cool-Season Gardening Tips & Tricks

Depending on where you live in the Southwest, your cool-season garden may be sown in the ground while it is still hitting 100°F in the middle of the day! Hard to get excited about gardening when it takes a gallon of sunblock and two gallons of water to simply venture outdoors. Remember, early in the morning and late in the afternoon are dandy times to garden. For those in the upper elevations, you may sow seed of autumn kale, a cool-season crop, in July or August—in the middle of the warm season. Not a problem with a little planning.

Put yourself in a seed's place. Soil temperature can be more critical to livelihood than air temperature. Once tender young leaves emerge from the soil, heat or frost are more of an issue.

Some plants need warm soils to germinate, but then grow better in cool temperatures—lettuce and cole crops are two examples—and such plants are ideal for an autumn garden. Note that if you plant warm-season crops into soil that is too cold, they often rot instead of grow, but the reverse is rarely the case.

Plants listed in this cool-season section of the book grow best during the cooler parts of the year. If the weather (and soil) is too warm, they may germinate but fail to thrive, or worse, wither away. If you look at the origin of most of the crops in this section, you will note that many are from northern or eastern Europe or other similar cool parts of the world. Genetically they are well adapted to our cool season, but they may still struggle with our low humidity.

Planting Seeds Outside

Most of the cool-season plants do best if planted from seed sown directly in the garden. This is indicated in the individual plant profiles.

Do pay attention to planting depth mentioned in the plant profiles and on the seed packages. A tiny seed, like lettuce, does not have enough stored energy to push its baby leaves too far through the soil. Big pea seeds need to be planted deeper. The rule of thumb is to plant seeds twice as deep as the height of the seed when it lays flat on your palm.

Seed-starting mix is worth the money to help ensure gardening success. I have one bucket of each—dark and light. The dark seed-starter mix is to help warm the seeds in the cool months. The white sand "starting mix" reflects light and keeps the seed cool in the warm months. Another plus to seed-starter soils is that they are generally lighter weight than actual garden soil, which makes it easier for sprouting seedlings to emerge.

Keep seeds moist when they are sprouting. This seems a no-brainer, but is critical in our arid climate. Twice a day water in summer is not out of line for seeds sprouting. My husband and I plan our vacation schedules so that I can be home during seed-sprouting time. Once the young plants have two to three sets of true leaves, they can stand a less frequent watering.

Planting Transplants

There are a variety of reasons to plant transplants instead of seed.

Some plants are easier to grow from transplants due to soil temperatures. Cool soils in the upper elevations in early spring can retard growth. While tiny seedlings are emerging from such cold soil, fungal attack can be a real issue. Transplants have grown past this problem.

Some plants are easier to grow from transplants due to space. Think how much of a crop you want and how much space you have available. I could freeze and use about a quarter acre of broccoli, but I don't have that much space, so a four-pack from the nursery has to suffice.

Some plants are easier to grow from transplants due to their nature. Onions grow best from "sets."

Some cool-season plants simply can't be grown from transplants in parts of the Southwest. Sadly, it's because it's hard to get nurseries to respect the needs of the Southwestern gardener. Corporate headquarters "Back East" tells them that cilantro is planted in April, so that is when they offer the plants in Phoenix. The cilantro promptly dies and discourages the budding gardener from ever trying to garden again. This book aims to prevent that problem!

Cool-Season Continual Harvest

If you plan and plant with attention, you can harvest your cool-season crops over a long period of time. Radishes are a good example of a crop you want only a few of at a time! Succession planting is the key. Succession planting is the process of planting the same plant, in successive weeks, through the growing season. Beets, carrots, chard, choy, kale, and lettuce join the radish on the list of good candidates for succession planting.

Harvesting

Most crops are ready at a specific time, as indicated by their "days to maturity." That doesn't mean that you can't eat some of them when they are small and tender. A number of beet varieties are just as tasty at 1-inch diameter as they are at 3-inch diameter.

Use days to maturity as your guide. They should be clearly indicated on the seed package or transplant label, and will help you when planning your succession planting as well as your seasonal rotation. Since this book is divided into five growing zones (covering fourteen USDA zones) you will need to keep the information on what you planted and when it matures at your fingertips. But!

But. Some crops in this cool-season section can be left in the soil in certain growing zones. In the Cool Highlands and High Desert, you can succession plant crops like carrots and kale during the autumn months and harvest them well into freezing weather, sometimes clear into December. The soil conditions can serve much like a refrigerator, cool and with medium humidity.

Parsnips, rutabagas, and turnips, when amply mulched with straw and a good snow cover can stay in the garden right through the winter, even in the Cold Mountains. (Some books say otherwise but this is common practice in parts of Vermont that are USDA Zone 4b, same as the Cold Mountain Zone here in the Southwest.)

Some plants, like broccoli, cabbage, and cauliflower, need to be harvested when they are ready, no fudging, no storing them in the garden. Others, like arugula and lettuce become bitter at the end of their season. In general this is because they are using their stored sugars to send up flower stalks, set seed, and go to the great compost heap in the sky.

Cover Crops

If you are not going to garden all year around, consider cover cropping. This is the practice of planting a beneficial plant such as a nitrogen-fixing legume in the portion of the garden you are not using at the time. Some good cover crops for our area include alfalfa, field peas, lentils, or buckwheat. Let these plants grow until they are about to flower then cut them down and compost them or feed them to chickens.

In the Low Desert, you may choose to only have a cool-season garden (and not garden in the summer). In this case your cover crop might be the native tepary beans. If you snowbird away in summer, why not toss out some tepary seed and see if it works?

Even if you do not cover crop, consider covering your garden. Our Southwestern winds can blow away a tremendous amount of good garden soil when you are not looking. Do not cover with plastic! That could solarize the soil and kill the beneficial microbes.

Crop Rotation

As you read the plant profiles, you will notice that some plants need to be moved where they grow in the garden each year. This is because these crops

are highly susceptible to soil-borne diseases. By moving where you plant them from year to year you avoid ever having the problem develop. (An ounce of prevention.) You may simply opt to do as I do, and grow these susceptible crops in large pots and provide them with new potting soil each year. The old soil gets dug in around the fruit trees, which are not susceptible to the same pathogens, and the trees are highly appreciative of my "recycling."

Cole crops like broccoli need to be planted in a different area of the garden each year.

ARUGULA
(Eruca sativa, also sold as *Eruca versicaria)*

Arugula goes by many names, including salad rocket, roquette, rugula, and garden rocket. It has rocketed into popularity in recent years as American palates demand more than plain iceberg lettuce in their salads. This member of the mustard family is an annual green that thrives during cool weather. In flavor it can be mild to peppery sharp, depending mostly on seed origin. Select what pleases your palate. Mature arugula plants are hardy to around 18°F, but newly planted seed will need frost protection. The white flowers are edible, but once the plants start to bolt (send up flower stalks) they are at the end of their life cycle. Be sure to save some seed of what you grew because it will do best for you in your garden with your care next year.

■ *Recommended Varieties*

'Wasabi' arugula is perhaps the sharpest and does well in the Southwest. For a milder flavor, plant 'Rustic' or 'Italian.' 'Astro' is heat tolerant, and may survive into the summer in Middle and Low Desert in partial shade. The seed sold as "wild arugula" is a different species (*Diplotaxis tenuifolia*) than *Eruca* or "salad arugula," and features a more spicy flavor. Luckily, this "wild arugula" will grow much the same as *Eruca* species. Consider some of both if you wish. It is always fun to experiment if you have enough growing space.

■ *When and Where to Plant*

Temperature: Arugula germinates best if soil temperatures are cool, from 40°F to 60°F. The plants grow best when soil temperatures are 50°F to 75°F, thus arugula grows best in cool weather, and appreciates a straw mulch to keep roots cool. It will survive higher temperatures but warmer season harvests will be spicy!

Plant: In the Low and Middle Desert regions, plant in September or October for harvest through March. In higher zones, plant in spring right around the last frost date for summer harvest. Successive plantings are not required unless you use a great deal of arugula.

Soil: Plants thrive in deep, fertile soil with lots of organic matter. The best pH is 6.0 to 7.5. It does well in containers. If a summer crop, consider terra cotta pots that allow moisture evaporation and help keep roots cool.

Sun: Full sun to partial shade in lower elevations.

■ *How to Plant*

Starting seeds indoors: You can start seeds indoors year-round if you prefer working with transplants in the garden bed.

Planting outside: Soak the seeds overnight before planting outside for faster germination.

■ *How to Grow*

Water: Keep soil moist for best germination and milder flavor. Arugula needs steady moisture, particularly as the weather warms, to help keep it from bolting.

Fertilizer: Sidedress with a balanced fertilizer (10-10-10, for example) once a month to encourage steady leaf production. Do not fertilize during potential frost months in the lower elevations.

Pest control: White flies may appear at the end of the growing season when plants are stressed. This is an indicator that it is time to harvest what you have left before the flies spread through the garden. Flea beetles may also strike arugula toward the end of the season. You can use floating row covers to control these pests, or harvest everything to discourage the pests. Do not compost insect-infested plants because unless you get your bin hot enough to kill any eggs you only multiply the pests for next year.

■ *When and How to Harvest*

Arugula is cut and come again. Young leaves are tender and mild, while older leaves are spicier and better for braising. Use scissors to cut the leaves at the base of the plant. Do not pull up the entire plant until the end of the season.

Mix arugula with other salad greens.

BEET *(Beta vulgaris,* Crassa Group*)*

Beets are primarily a root crop, but their tops—the leaves, called beet greens—are tasty and nutritious, too. (If you take a look at the scientific name of chard, you will see they are the same species.) Young beet greens are great in salads, while the larger greens you get when harvesting beets taste good braised or steamed. Beets need full sun and loose soil to form good roots. As with all root crops, beets grow best when sown directly into the garden, rather than planted as transplants.

If your only experience with beets is pickled varieties on the salad bar, you're missing out. Beets taste delicious when roasted. You can also grate raw beets onto your salads. Kids love beets ripe and raw because they are naturally sweet. (Think sugar beets!) Select from many colors, including traditional magenta, white, golden, and striped varieties.

■ *Recommended Varieties*

Select 'Early Wonder' or 'Bull's Blood' for Low and Middle Desert, and for short season cold Mountain growing. High Desert and Cool Highlands consider 'Ruby Queen', 'Early Wonder', and 'Red Ace'. All zones should try

Both the tops and the roots of beets can be eaten.

'Chioggia', delightfully candy-striped on the inside or 'Golden', a yellow variety. If you plan to store your beets, 'Winter Keeper' is good.

When and Where to Plant

Temperature: Beets germinate best when soil temperatures are 60°F to 75°F. The plants grow best when soil temperatures are 65°F to 75°F (mulch may be required).

Plant: In the Mountains, High Plateau, and High Desert, sow seeds three weeks before last frost. In the High Plateau and High Desert, sow again August 1 to 31. Sow seeds September 1 to October 15 in the Low and Middle Desert.

Soil: Beets need deep, loose, fertile soils with a pH of 6.5 to 7.5. Deep containers, though not ideal, can work.

Sun: Full sun to very light shade.

How to Plant

Starting seeds indoors: Can be done but root production may be marred.

Planting outside: Sow seeds outside 2 inches apart and ½ inch deep. Thinning will be required but is easily done with sharp scissors. Use these thinned "micro-greens" in salads.

How to Grow

Water: Beets need regular, even moisture to avoid scab, a condition in which brown, raised patches form on the outsides of the roots.

Fertilizer: Pre-fertilize the soil with ample compost prior to planting. A monthly application of balanced fertilizer (10-10-10) in any non-frost month will improve root production.

Pest control: Beets have no major pests in the Southwest.

When and How to Harvest

To harvest beet greens for salads while keeping the roots growing, use scissors to cut no more than one-quarter of the leaves from one plant at any time. To grow beets for this dual purpose, it is best to use small beet greens only as an addition to salads, not as the only green in a salad bowl.

Size of home-grown beets is not a good indicator of readiness for harvest, and if you leave them in the soil too long they will become woody and tough. It is best to harvest beets by the days to maturity as listed on their seed package (generally after sixty days growing). But, if you grow beets in the winter garden and cold or frost has slowed their growth cycle, you will need to pull one every few days near the harvest date and test for fully developed sweetness, texture, and flavor. If you are harvesting beets for storage (in a root cellar, for example) leave the leaves on after harvest, and dry the roots on a screen in a cool dark area.

BROCCOLI & CAULIFLOWER

(Brassica oleracea, Italica Group*)* and
(Brassica oleracea, Botrytis Group*)*

Broccoli and cauliflower are kissing cousins, and both are "cole" crops that are grown for undeveloped heads of flowers. (Cole crops include many other species of *Brassica*, including cabbage for cole slaw, kohlrabi, and more.) These two *Brassicas* are filled with vitamins and minerals—not to mention awesome flavor! In most of the Southwest you can grow at least one crop per season and occasionally two. Be sure to move the area of the garden where you plant your broccoli and similar cole crops each year to prevent soil-borne diseases from infecting your plants. Rotating crops is solid gardening practice but is especially necessary with all the *Brassicas*.

■ Recommended Varieties

BROCCOLI: For the winter garden in Low and Middle Desert consider 'Waltham 29', 'Fiesta', and 'Nutri-bud'. They feature good cold tolerance and ample production of side shoots. For the upper elevations 'DeCicco' ('Di Cicco'), 'Emperor', 'Fiesta', and 'Green Duke' are suggested. Heirlooms for the Southwest (featuring lime-green spirals of florets) include 'Romanesco' and 'Veronica'.

CAULIFLOWER: 'Snow Crown' tolerates swings in the weather for Low and Middle Desert growing. For all locations consider 'Amazing' or the purple-colored 'Violet Queen'.

■ When and Where to Plant

Temperature: These germinate best when soil temperatures are 60°F to 75°F.

Soil: Soil composition is less important than pH. These cole crops will grow in clay or sandy soils, but soil pH should be 6.0 to 7.0. If the soil pH is above 7.5, add

Successive crops of broccoli can be grown throughout the cool season.

ample compost or even coffee grounds to help acidify soil.

Sun: Full sun to very light shade in lower elevations.

How to Plant

Starting seeds indoors: Start seeds indoors at least sixty days before you want to transplant plants outside. Both of these take three to ten days to germinate and about a month to grow to transplantable size.

To get white heads on your cauliflower, tie the top of the leaves together over the first small curds.

Planting outside: For High Plateau and Mountain growing, harden off your transplants before planting them outside in spring. For Low and Middle Desert, it is easy to direct-sow a fall crop and get good results. Leave 12 to 18 inches between transplants, or thin seedlings (snip with scissors) to this spacing after direct-seeding. Thinnings are edible.

How to Grow

Water: Keep evenly moist throughout the growing season.

Fertilizer: These cole crops require both nitrogen and phosphorous to form good crowns. Once plants are 6 inches tall, apply a balanced fertilizer every three to four weeks in nonfrost months.

Pest control: All cole crops are susceptible to a variety of pests, including cabbage whites, cabbage loopers, and flea beetles. Use floating row covers when flying insects are active. Neem oil can be used well before harvest.

When and How to Harvest

BROCCOLI: Cut the center flower head when it is still dark green and tight. When the head starts to loosen and turn yellow, it's too late. If you're growing a variety that produces side shoots, leave the rest of the plant in the garden for up to two months. If the variety is primarily grown for the large center head, cut the heads and pull up the rest of the plant to make room for your next vegetable crop.

CAULIFLOWER: As cauliflower nears its "days to maturity" start checking for the formation of tiny heads. Once they begin to form, cover the head with a scrap of cardboard (or pluck and use a lower leaf) to ensure good head color. Once heads are ready, pull up the entire plant.

CARROT *(Daucus carota* var. *sativus)*

Once you've eaten a carrot you grew yourself, you will never want to go back to the bland, bitter, soapy-tasting carrots from the grocery store. Carrots have splendid flavor, but you'd never know it if you didn't pull one out of your own garden and eat it. Carrots need patience to grow—they take a long time to germinate. If your garden is sun challenged, you can grow carrots (and parsnips) with as little as four hours of sun a day. They do need sandy, well-drained soil, so you could grow them in deep containers, one way to get the soil just right.

For best results, plant carrots in soil that is loose and free of rocks.

■ *Recommended Varieties*

For Southwestern soils and containers, plan on short carrots, like 'Little Finger', 'Thumbelina', 'Danvers Half Long', 'Nantes Half Long', or my favorite, 'Kinko 6'. Colorful and longer carrots, such as 'Spartan Bonus', 'Scarlet Nantes', 'Apache', 'Red Cored Chanteny', or 'Orlando Gold', a yellow variety, can also be grown here. I am looking for a good rich purple carrot to grow alongside the golden ones so I can serve carrots in the colors of my husband's favorite football team.

■ *When and Where to Plant*

Temperature: Carrots will germinate when the soil temperature is 60°F to 75°F. They'll grow best at soil temperatures of 60°F to 70°F, so consider straw mulch in the summer garden.

Plant: In September in the Low and Middle Desert. Plant after last frost in the upper elevations.

Soil: The most important part of growing carrots is getting the soil right for them. They require acidic soil with a pH of 5.5 to 6.5. The soil must also be loose, well-drained, and free of rocks. In the Southwest, a raised bed or deep container is ideal to grow carrots.

Sun: Full sun to part shade.

■ *How to Plant*

Starting seeds indoors: Like many root crops, carrots do not transplant well.

Planting outside: Sow seed ¼ to ½ inch deep. In Low and Middle Desert, shade cloth over the row or deep pot will help cool the soil for germination, as will a reflective layer of light-colored sand over the top of the seed. In upper elevations, cover seeds with seed-starting mix, and keep the seeds moist while germinating. Be patient! It can take up to three weeks for carrots to germinate, and the soil must stay evenly moist the whole time you're waiting.

■ *How to Grow*

Water: Keep moist while germinating and keep evenly watered during the growing season.

Thinning: Use sharp scissors to thin carrots to 1 inch apart after the first true (lacy-looking) leaves appear. When plants are 3 inches tall, thin to 3-inch spacing.

Fertilizer: For sweeter carrots, feed the leaves with a nitrogen fertilizer once a month.

Pest control: Carrots are fairly pest free in the home garden. The larvae of the swallowtail butterfly will eat the tops sometimes, but this rarely causes enough damage to worry about.

■ *When and How to Harvest*

Carrots take sixty to seventy-five days to grow to maturity but may take longer in the winter garden. You can start to harvest them as soon as the roots turn orange (or red or yellow, depending on the variety). To harvest, grasp the leafy top as near the root as possible and pull directly upward. Don't harvest them all at once! Work your way along the row, harvesting what you want to eat at the time of harvest. If it is cool, you can leave carrots in the ground for about a month after maturity.

PARSNIP (*Pastinaca sativa*)

Parsnips not only look like carrots, they are very close relatives that require the same growing conditions as carrots, so I mention them here. Parsnips are best eaten cooked, which develops their sweet, buttery smooth flavor. Roast them, put them in soups and stews, or mash them like potatoes for a less starchy taste treat. Parsnips are an often overlooked vegetable, so there are not many varieties. 'Javelin' is one that does well and is cold tolerant for overwintering in the Southwest. Start and grow just like carrots.

CHARD *(Beta vulgaris,* Cicla Group*)*

With colors as brilliant as a Southwest sunset, chard is a beautiful plant for any garden. Also called Swiss chard, this is technically a beet, but you don't grow it for the roots. It has been bred to produce colorful and tasty stems and leaves. Good in salads, for cooking, or even pickling, chard is a handy plant to go along with its beauty. Indeed, chard is so pretty that it doesn't have to be contained in the vegetable garden. If you're short on space, grow this lovely vegetable in the perennial flower garden. It will look right at home. Chard can become a perennial in USDA Zones 7 and above, but I have found it is not worth the water and garden space to keep it alive through the summer—the leaves become tough and fibrous and there are a variety of tasty warm weather greens waiting to take the space.

■ *Recommended Varieties*

'Umania' is a slow-to-bolt Japanese variety that can take the fluctuating temperatures of a winter garden in the Low, Middle, and High Desert.

Swiss chard is pretty enough to grow in a flower garden.

For all zones consider any of these: 'Bright Lights', 'Fantasia Orange', 'Golden Sunrise', 'Magenta Sunset', 'Rainbow', or 'Ruby Red'. Seed catalogs are fun. If you see another variety that interests you, consider trying it, but bear in mind our unique Southwestern growing conditions. Larger-leaved varieties, like 'Fordhook Giant' do not do well in our low humidity.

When and Where to Plant

Temperature: Chard grows best in cool temperatures.

Plant: Outside after last frost in upper elevations, and in the winter garden in lower elevations. Can be grown in containers on the patio.

Soil: Rich, well-drained acidic soil is best, with ample compost and pH of 6.0 to 7.0.

Sun: Full sun to partial shade.

How to Plant

Starting seeds indoors: Not necessary, but if you wish, start seeds four weeks prior to planting.

Planting outside: Sow seeds directly out into the garden, one seed every 2 inches, ½ inch deep (thin later). You can soak seeds overnight before planting. Plant transplants at least 8 inches apart. Chard plants can get fairly large, so some gardeners prefer block planting as is done with lettuce.

How to Grow

Water: Keep chard evenly moist.

Fertilizer: For best production, fertilize with a balanced fertilizer every two to four weeks during the nonfreezing months.

Pest control: Use insecticidal soap to take care of any aphids that might appear. Leaf miners are inside the leaves, and thus the only recourse is to cut and entirely discard any infested leaves.

When and How to Harvest

You can start harvesting leaves of chard as soon as the plant has at least four or five leaves. Take the outermost leaves first, and allow the inner leaves to grow and provide sugars for the plant. Use a sharp knife, scissors, or hand pruners to cut the leaf stalks at the soil level.

CHINESE CABBAGE & CHOY CABBAGE

(Brassica rapa, Pekinensis Group*)* and
(Brassica rapa, Chinensis Group*)*

Choy (and Chinese cabbage) can be planted in blocks instead of rows.

I prefer Chinese cabbage over European cabbage in my garden for a number of reasons—it takes less space per plant, has a milder flavor, and produces none of the "gassy" side-effects of European cabbage. There are two main types of Chinese cabbages, "open-head, or "loose-head," looking somewhat like a lacy Romaine lettuce, and "head" or "Nappa-type," with outer leaves that wrap over the head. Chinese cabbage is the same species as turnips (*Brassica rapa* ssp. *rapa*) and broccoli-Raab (*Brassica rapa,* Ruvo Group), but has been bred over the centuries for the leaves instead of roots or flower buds, and also to be sweeter and milder in flavor.

Bok Choy, Pak Choy, and the smaller Baby Choys such as Joy Choy or Mei Quing Choy—just to name a few of the choys—all are delightful in flavor. The larger choy varieties offer two vegetables in one. The crunchy crisp stems are sweeter and less stringy than celery, and can be cooked like asparagus. The leafy portion is, to my palate, far better in taste and texture than chard, kale, or spinach. Choys come with your choice of green or white stems. Choys have a tidy rosette of upright leaves and grow to various sizes, depending on cultivar. If you enjoy greens, the smaller choys are especially worth what little space they require in the garden. If you have kids who don't like broccoli (a closely related vegetable), consider serving choy, especially the sweeter, smaller varieties.

Both Choy and Chinese cabbage are grown in much the same manner and both can be block planted.

■ *Recommended Cultivars & Varieties*

For the Southwest select the smaller, more heat-tolerant varieties that mature quickly (thirty to sixty days). This will reduce water consumed to produce your crop and quickly free up garden space for another crop of the same or some other vegetable.

CHINESE CABBAGE, LOOSE-HEAD: 'Hiroshima' and 'Maruba Santoh' are both quick to mature.

CHINESE CABBAGE HEAD-TYPE: 'Mini Kisaku 50 Hybrid', 'Tenderheart Hybrid'.

CHOYS: 'Green Fortune', 'Joi Choy', 'Mei Quin Choi', 'Petite Star', 'Shanghai', 'Tsatsoi'.

■ *When and Where to Plant*

Temperature: Germination soil temperatures, 75°F to 80°F (night air temperatures above 50°F).

Plant: In Cool Mountains, plant after last frost. In Cool Plateau and High Desert areas, you may be able to sow two crops, one just after last frost, and the second crop six weeks before date of first frost in fall. In Middle and Lower Desert gardens, plant in fall for winter consumption, plus you can plant a second crop of non-heading varieties from February into mid-March.

Soil: Rich loamy soil with a pH of 6.0 to 7.0 is best. I have grown them in pure desert soil but they were stunted. Can be grown in containers on the patio.

■ *How to Plant*

Starting seeds indoors: Not ideal due to shallow, delicate root system, but if you are careful transplanting, start seedlings four to six weeks before last frost.

Planting outside: Sow seed ¼ to ½ inch deep. Consider block planting, or thin to 8 to 18 inches apart depending on type. These thinnings can go into salads or stir-fry.

■ *How to Grow*

Water: Moderate and even.

Fertilizer: Provide ample nitrogen for good leaf production. Like all cool-season greens, small amounts of general fertilizer every two to three weeks works better than large amounts less often.

Pest control: This is in the same genus as other cole crops, and the same care applies. Rotate cole crops away from soil you planted any cole crops in for at least one year. Remove and discard (do not compost) any cole crop roots. Flea beetles can be controlled with floating row covers.

■ *When and How to Harvest*

You can start using these delightful greens as soon as they are large enough to use. Thus block planting and thinning through the season to help them form into upright plants makes wonderful sense. Fall crops can be stored for several weeks wrapped in newspaper in the root cellar.

COLE CROPS

While all of these vegetables look very different in the garden, they are all the same species, just like the Irish Wolfhound and Dachshund are the same species (*Canis lupus familiaris*). Unlike the dogs mentioned, the care, feeding, and even "health issues" of these variety of *Brassicas* is much the same, so I have placed them together here. All of these cole crops, eaten fresh out of the garden, are sweet, flavorful, and generally not "gassy" at all. Science reveals that once picked, the cell compounds begin to break down, may become bitter, and can cause "gastric discomfort." If this is an issue in your family, harvest and enjoy without storing.

■ *Recommended Varieties*

BRUSSELS SPROUTS (*Brassica oleracea*, Gemmifera Group): Plants get tall, and can blow over in our gusty winds. I place a tomato cage around the plants when the plants are still small to avoid this problem. 'Long Island Improved' is a taller variety good in the Mountains and Highlands. In High and Middle Desert regions 'Jade Cross' works well. The Low Desert does not have the frost required for sweet Brussels sprouts.

The sprouts of Brussels sprouts develop along the plant stem. You harvest from the bottom up.

CABBAGE (*Brassica oleracea*, Capitata Group): 'Golden Acre' and 'Red Acre' are ideal for desert winter gardens, and work well in the upper elevations. Also consider 'Savoy Ace' and 'Ruby Ball.'

KOHLRABI (*Brassica oleracea*, Gongylodes Group): You may have never tried kohlrabi before, but I find it well worth the garden space. The crunchy, juicy swollen basal stem can be peeled and used instead of chips for dips, grated for slaw, or cooked like potatoes or turnips. White, green, or purple flesh as you wish. For all zones select from 'White Vienna', 'Early Purple Vienna', 'Blaro', or 'Grand Duke'.

■ *When and Where to Plant*

Temperature: Cole crops germinate in soil temperatures of 60°F to 75°F. Air temperatures need to remain below 90°F to keep the plant from bolting. You can start growing them in the warmer days of summer (in lower elevations) but they will need cool weather in order to mature.

Plant: In the Low and Middle Desert plant seeds outside in August or September and let them grow and mature throughout the fall and winter for spring harvest. In the High Desert plant transplants outside in early March. You can seed again in early July. In the Cool Highlands plant transplants outside in April and as seed in late May. You can plant seed again in July for an autumn harvest. In the High Mountains plant transplants outside in late May. You may be able to get an autumn crop with seeds planted in July.

Soil: Soil pH should be 6.5 to 7.5. Add ample compost prior to planting.

Sun: Full sun.

How to Plant

Starting seeds indoors: Start six weeks ahead (at least four weeks are needed). Seedlings will need to harden off before planting—the plants need to get used to the cold (in spring) and the heat (in summer) before planting.

Planting outside: Plant transplants 16 to 18 inches apart. Direct-sow seed ¼ inch deep at 6-inch spacing. Thin seedlings to 18-inch spacing after plants are 6 inches tall.

How to Grow

Water: Keep evenly moist throughout the growing season.

Fertilizer: Add compost to the soil before planting. Fertilize with a balanced fertilizer once a month in the nonfrost months.

Pest control: Cutworms can affect transplants. To protect young plants, wrap the bottom 3 to 4 inches of stem with foil or smear with petroleum jelly. Cabbage looper moths and cabbage worms can be treated with insecticidal soap. Floating row covers are also an option if you are beset with flying pests.

When and How to Harvest

Brussels sprouts mature from the bottom up. Harvest each sprout with clippers as it reaches ¾ to 1inch in diameter. Alternatively, harvest the entire stalk and store on the stalk, hung upside down, in a root cellar for up to forty-five days.

For cabbage, once the head is head-like instead of a mass of leaves, and feels firm, it is ready to pick; the smaller the more tasty. Use pruners or a knife to cut off the head just below the base.

Harvest kohlrabi by pulling up the entire plant. Start harvesting when the stems are 1 inch in diameter, and continue to harvest until the stems are 3 inches in diameter. If you let them grow larger, they will be woody, fibrous, and tough.

FENNEL *(Foeniculum vulgare var. azoricum* and *Foeniculum vulgare var. dulce)*

There are two types of fennel, the bulb-forming Florence fennel (*Foeniculum vulgare* var. *azoricum*), and bronze fennel (*Foeniculum vulgare* var. *dulce*), grown primarily for its tasty and attractive leaves. Florence fennel is delectable used fresh instead of chips for dips, or it can be cooked in a wide variety of ways (like with roasted roots—yum!). I use bronze fennel in salads, and add leaves to stir fry. The seeds of either fennel are dried as an herb, especially popular in European cooking. Fennel is a splendid butterfly plant, highly attractive to both larvae and adult swallowtail butterflies. Since the two-tailed swallowtail is the official state butterfly of Arizona, I always plant extra fennel to share with them and attract them into my garden.

◼ *Recommended Cultivars & Varieties*

BULBING FENNEL: Heirloom 'Finocchio' works well as do 'Orion', 'Perfection', and 'Zefa Fino'.

BRONZE FENNEL: Generally sold without cultivar name, although 'Purpureum' is one to try.

◼ *When and Where to Plant*

Temperature: Sow seeds outside when the soil temperature is at least 60°F.

Soil: Fennel needs well-drained, nutrient-rich soil with a pH of 6.5 to 7.5. Both fennels grow well in deep containers.

Sun: Full sun to partial shade at lower elevations.

◼ *How to Plant*

Starting seeds indoors: Not recommended; fennel has a taproot, which makes it difficult to transplant. If you need to start seeds indoors (in the Cold Mountains), plant them in a peat or coir pot that can be planted directly outside without disturbing the plant roots.

Planting outside: Sow seeds outdoors, 4 inches apart, and barely cover with seed-starting mix. Thin seeds to 8 inches apart when plants are 4 inches tall. Use the plants you thin to flavor salads.

◼ *How to Grow*

Water: Fennel is a low-water plant, but you'll need to water it if it doesn't rain at least once a week. Bronze fennel over-summered for three years in a shady location in my Middle Desert garden.

Fertilizer: No extra fertilizer is needed, but bulbing fennel does better with general fertilizer once a month in any nonfrost month.

The leaves of bronze fennel are edible, and refreshing to chew while you work in the garden.

Pest control: Fennel is fairly pest free. Swallowtail butterfly larvae use the foliage for food, but they have never decimated my crop. Let these caterpillars munch. The plants will recover.

When and How to Harvest

Harvest leaves from either type of fennel with scissors as needed for use. Harvest seed by cutting off the entire flower stalk after the seed is set and before it falls. Invert the stalks into a large paper sack. Dry at least two more weeks after stalks appear dry before cleaning and storage of the seed.

Harvest Florence fennel bulbs when they are the sweetest, just as they start to convert stored starch into sugar for flowers. Wait until flower buds form, cut the buds off, wait a few more days, and pull up the entire plant. Toss the foliage into the composter and enjoy the bulbs soon after harvest—raw, steamed, sautéed, or roasted.

GARLIC *(Allium sativum* varieties)

Garlic is so incredibly more flavorful when grown at home you may never buy supermarket garlic again. Originally from Asia, garlic is easy to grow in the Southwest because it appreciates our low humidity—but you do have to select the correct variety and plant at the correct time. For the garlic bulb to split into multiple cloves, it needs at least forty days of weather under 40°F. For this reason, garlic is a fall- and winter-grown vegetable in much of our region. If you can purchase garlic "seed" bulbs locally, all the better—you're more likely to have success with your plantings. Do not simply plant supermarket garlic; you will be underwhelmed with the results.

■ *Recommended Cultivars & Varieties*

Along with many cultivars, garlic is divided into two major varieties, based on day-length dependency: softneck (*Allium sativum* var. *sativum*) or hardneck (*Allium sativum* var. *ophioscorodon*). In our area, it's best to plant softneck varieties. Lucky for us, softneck is easy to grow, with plump cloves, longest storage ability and is the best kind for braiding.

'Silverskin' is an all-purpose workhorse variety that grows well in all of our Southwest gardens and is somewhat heat tolerant. It's a good choice for beginners and stores nine to twelve months. 'California Early' (developed by California growers) is milder than 'Silverskin' with large cloves that slip apart easily. Also consider the reddish purple varieties 'Ajo Rojo' or 'Chinatown Xian Early'.

Elephant garlic (*Allium ampeloprasum*) is not true garlic, it's technically a leek, but with a garlic taste. The common name comes from the giant size of the basal bulb. It is less cold-hardy than true garlic, making it ideal for the Low and Middle Desert gardens.

Once harvested, garlic can be stored in a cool, dry location.

■ *When and Where to Plant*

Temperature: In all five regions plant in September. The lower regions will harvest in spring; the upper three regions will harvest in summer. Low- and Middle Desert can plant as late as January.

Soil: Well-drained soil is required. Add sand if necessary. Soil pH should ideally be from 6.5 to 7.5 for these varieties. Add compost to the soil prior to planting.

Sun: Full sun.

■ *How to Plant*

Starting seeds indoors: It is easiest to start with cloves of garlic. The advanced gardener may like the challenge of growing from true seed. If so, start seeds indoors four to eight weeks before you plan to plant outdoors. You can sow eight to ten seeds per 4-inch pot and then tease apart the roots when you're ready to plant outside.

Planting outside: Plant garlic cloves 1 inch deep and 4 to 6 inches apart. Sow seeds ¼ inch deep, 2 inches apart outside and thin (into the salad bowl) to 6 inches after plants have two sets of leaves. When planting transplants, harden off before planting.

■ *How to Grow*

Water: Keep the soil moist during the first four weeks after planting—this is when the garlic cloves are growing roots. In upper three zones no further water is needed until spring. Then, resume watering once leaves begin to appear. In the two lower zones, keep soil evenly moist with regular water throughout the growing cycle. At the end of the life cycle, decrease watering to allow the bulbs to dry out.

Fertilizer: If you added compost to the soil before planting, you do not need to fertilize while the plants are growing. If you didn't add compost, top dress the area where garlic is planted with an organic fertilizer. Avoid fertilizer during frost months.

Pest control: Garlic plants are fairly pest tolerant. In fact, garlic is used in many organic pest control products.

■ *When and How to Harvest*

Garlic is ready to harvest when the tops start dying back. When you see the leaves start to turn yellow, stop watering the bulbs. Once the tops have died back, use a trowel to gently dig up the bulbs. (Unless you have ample compost and sand, you can't pull the bulbs up by the leaves.) Store garlic by braiding the tops together and hanging in a cool, dry location, not in the refrigerator.

GREENS, COOL-SEASON

Greens are the ideal cool-season crop, and there are so many to choose from! Kale, chard, and the cole crops have their own pages in this book, so here is where I have lumped the greens with similar care requirements. Cool-season leafy vegetables need the right soil temperature to germinate and then they need the short days (and long nights) associated with fall, winter, and early spring to stay vegetative—producing leaves but not flowers. Once the weather heats up, these greens will become bitter and bolt (begin to flower). Pollinators appreciate the flowers, so if you have the space, leave the plants (plus then you can harvest your own seed for next year).

Use scissors to snip off lettuce leaves, and they will grow back.

■ *Recommended Varieties*

CRESS: If you have a fish pond or water garden, put in a pot of cress with just the bottom inch of the pot submerged. Upland cress (*Barbarea verna*), curly cress (*Lepidium sativum*), garden cress (*Tropaeolum majus*), and watercress (*Nasturtium officinale*) are all good cool-season greens grown this way.

EUROPEAN SPINACH (*Spinaceia oleracea*): Any of the smaller-leaved varieties do well in the Southwest, but with all these other, far more tasty, greens available I do not waste the space.

LETTUCE (*Lactuca sativa*): There are four types of lettuce: crisphead, butterhead, romaine, and looseleaf. Looseleaf and butterhead are most successful in the Southwest. Romaine and crisphead don't do so well in our heat and alkaline soils. 'Black-Seeded Simpson' and 'Simpson Elite' are two good green-leaf varieties. 'Red Sails' and 'Lolla Rosa' are easy-to-grow red-leaf varieties. Try 'Buttercrunch' if you want a heading lettuce.

MACHE (*Valerianella locusta*): This is also called corn salad or lamb's lettuce. Once you grow this you will never eat lettuce again. It simply melts in your mouth.

MESCLUN: Mixed seed that generally includes many of these greens mentioned here. Grow in blocks and harvest handfuls for salads, generally within three weeks of sowing.

MICROGREENS: Mixed seed that generally includes many of these greens mentioned here. Cut and consume when they are 3 to 4 inches tall.

MIZUNA (*Brassica rapa* var. *japonica*): Has a mild mustard flavor and is good in salads or cooked.

MUSTARD (*Brassica juncea*): Southwest's own 'Mostaza Roja' is mild enough for salads or used as a cooked green. Avoid any variety with "giant" in its name; they do not do well here.

ORACH (*Atriplex hortensis*): Also called wild spinach, I prefer it over European spinach as it has a sweeter flavor and no gritty feel. 'Magenta Magic' offers lovely color to your salad.

SORREL (*Rumex acetosa*): Eaten raw or cooked, adds a tangy lemony flavor to food. May be a perennial with a carrot-like taproot in the upper elevations; plant as an annual in desert gardens.

TATSOI (*Brassica rapa* var. *narinosa*): Has a mild mustard flavor, and is good in salads or cooked.

■ *When and Where to Plant*

Temperature: Cool-season greens will germinate in soil temperatures of 45°F to 75°F. In desert gardens, greens are for winter, in upper elevations, early spring. Low Desert, sow seed outdoors after November 1 until

February 1. Middle Desert, sow in October. High Desert, sow in September. Cool Highlands and Cold Mountains, sow outdoors right around the last frost date.

Soil: All of these greens need a rich, well-drained soil, with a pH of 6.5 to 7.5. Add ample compost or aged manure to the soil before planting for healthy growth. Containers also work well.

Sun: Full to partial sun.

◼ *How to Plant*

Starting seeds indoors: You can start greens seeds indoors, especially if you live in the mountains. In other zones, it is easiest to grow from seed outdoors.

Planting outside: Sow seeds outdoors and cover with seed-starting mix or potting soil. Press the soil down and water. (Pressing the soil down helps keep the tiny seeds from floating away.) Thin to 4 inches after the plants have three sets of leaves. Thin to 12-inch spacing as the plants start to mature. Eat what you thin! Sow cut-and-come-again greens, like micro-greens, thickly—three seeds per inch.

Consider succession planting of these greens for continual harvest (see page 106).

◼ *How to Grow*

Water: Greens are not heavy drinkers, but keep the soil evenly moist for best flavor.

Fertilizer: Remember, "leaves love nitrogen." All leaf crops respond well to applications of well-composted chicken manure prior to planting. When temperatures are above 55°F you can use a nitrogen fertilizer every two weeks.

Pest control: The arid Southwest offers the home gardener few insect pests on greens (yet). Quail are notorious eaters of tender young greenery, and since I have neighbors who put out quail seed, I place a screen of chicken wire over the large pots I grow my greens in. This keeps the quail from eating the young plants, and they leave the larger leaves that grow up through the screen alone.

◼ *When and How to Harvest*

Harvest your greens using scissors to snip off leaves about ½ to 1 inch above the soil line, or at the stem for taller greens. Often, more leaves will grow. If you can, harvest in the morning when the water content of the leaves is highest. Invest in a good salad spinner to wash all your homegrown greens.

With a little planning, you can overwinter European spinach in warmer regions.

KALE *(Brassica oleracea,* Acephala Group*)*

Kale is easy to grow and a popular edible.

Here is yet another member of the cole crops—kale. Kale has become an "in" vegetable. Everyone is drinking kale smoothies, eating kale chips, and generally espousing the benefits of this leafy green vegetable. It's for good reason, though: kale is the most nutrient-dense vegetable per calorie you can eat. It's also easy to grow. Once you plant it, you can basically leave it alone and harvest leaves off the plants for months. Young leaves are tender enough to put in fresh salads, while larger leaves are perfect for soups and braised greens. For a tasty and healthy treat, prepare a large bunch of kale by removing the center ribs and tearing the leaves into 1- to 2-inch pieces. Place in a bowl with a sprinkle of salt, a bit of olive oil, and a generous soaking of flavored vinegar. You'll find yourself craving this delicious salad and searching for new flavored vinegars to try it with.

◼ Recommended Varieties

'Dwarf Siberian' and 'Dwarf Blue' are good for small gardens and containers in the upper elevations and in the winter gardens of the lower elevations. 'Lacinato' is both heat and cold tolerant, with dark, blue-green leaves. A highly adaptable variety, it can be grown almost all year long in the Southwest with summer shade at the lower elevations. 'Toscano' is a dinosaur-type kale (it has wrinkly leaves like wrinkly dinosaur skin). 'Red Russian' does well in the winter garden and the young leaves are great in salads. Also consider 'Green Curled Scotch', 'Early Siberian', 'Vates', 'Dwarf Blue Curled Scotch', and 'Blue Knight'.

When and Where to Plant

Temperature: Kale seeds will germinate in soil temperatures of 45°F to 95°F. That said, it grows best with cool daytime temperatures (60°F to 75°F).

Soil: For best flavor, add ample compost to the soil so pH is 6.0 to 7.0. Containers are fine for kale.

Sun: Full sun to partial shade.

How to Plant

Starting seeds indoors: Start seeds indoors six weeks before you want to transplant outdoors.

Planting outside: Plant seeds outside 3 inches apart and transplants 8 to 12 inches apart.

How to Grow

Water: Keep kale growing, thriving, and producing tender (not bitter and fibrous) leaves by watering consistently when the plants are actively growing.

Fertilizer: As with all green, leafy vegetables, kale needs ample nitrogen. Fertilize by sidedressing with an organic, slow-release fertilizer every three to four weeks during the growing season.

Pest control: Kale is more resistant to pests than other cole crops. Aphids can be a problem late in the season. Control these with insecticidal soap. Cabbage worms and cabbage looper caterpillars may also munch on kale. If you see the "worms," pick them off and drop them in a pail of soapy water. Some gardeners treat with *Bacillus thuringiensis* (*B.t.*) but this kills all butterflies, even the beneficial ones that pollinate other plants.

When and How to Harvest

Keep your scissors handy when harvesting kale. A sharp yank can cause the whole plant to come out of the ground. Cut small young leaves to use fresh in salads. Harvest the larger leaves for braising and stir-fry. Harvest from the bottom of the plant up, which lets inner leaves keep growing. You'll know when it's time to stop harvesting by the taste of the leaves. Once they get to be too stringy or woody, it's time to dig the plants up and make space in your garden for something else.

ONION & SCALLION
(Allium spp.)

Onions, and scallions, and shallots, oh my! They're so inexpensive to buy that you might wonder why you should bother growing them, but the flavor of a freshly harvested onion is incredible. Plus, if you select the right varieties,

they're easy to grow and need little care. I know a lady who lives in a neighborhood rigidly controlled by an HOA (home owners association). She grew a large crop of onions and garlic in her front yard. Nicely planted in curving "flower beds," her crop was part of her landscape—and she got no hassles from the HOA "Yard Patrol." You can grow onions from seeds, bulbs (also called sets), and transplants.

For easiest growth and storage, grow onions from sets to get a jump start on the season.

Bulbing onions (*Allium cepa*) are classified by the number of daylight hours required to get them to form bulbs. In Low, Middle, and High Desert plant short-day onions in the winter for early summer harvest. In the Cool Highlands and Cold Mountains plant intermediate-day onions in the spring for fall harvest.

Scallions, also called green onions, are "bunching onions" because they form leafy clusters, not large bulbs. They also do well in the Southwestern garden. Most scallions are *Allium cepa* var. *cepa*, but the Japanese bunching onion (*Allium fistulosum*), also called the red scallion, is now available.

Multiplier onions, including shallots, are different than bunching onions since they form many small bulbs. Technically they are *Allium cepa* var. *aggregatum*. Confusingly, some catalogs refer to them as "bunching onions" as well. When in doubt, use the scientific name.

◼ *Recommended Varieties*

BULBING ONIONS (*Allium cepa* var. *cepa*): Short-day (Desert zones) varieties: 'Texas Super Sweet', 'Yellow Granex', 'White Bermuda', 'White Granex', and 'Southern Belle Red'. Intermediate-day (Cool and Cold zones) varieties: 'Candy', 'Super Star', and 'Stockton Sweet Red'.

SCALLIONS (*Allium cepa* var. *cepa*): All areas can plant 'Parade' and 'Mini-purplette'.

MULTIPLIER ONIONS (*Allium cepa* var. *aggregatum*): For the three Desert zones, consider 'I'itoi'. For the upper elevations, 'Lisbon White', 'Red Baron', and the Heirloom 'Red Torpedo' do well.

SHALLOTS (*Allium cepa* var. *aggregatum*): Short day (Desert zones): 'Santee' and 'Matador'. Intermediate day (Cool and Cold zones): 'Picador', 'Camelot', and 'Ambition'.

When and Where to Plant

Soil: Onions grow best in loamy soils with a pH of 6.5 to 7.5. You'll have to fertilize more if you are growing onions in sandy soil.

Sun: Full sun to light shade.

How to Plant

Starting seeds indoors: Start onion seeds indoors six weeks before you plan to transplant them outdoors.

Planting outside: If planting seeds, you can sow up to four weeks earlier than if you are planting transplants. Plant bunching onions close together (2 inches apart) and bulbing onions 6 inches apart.

How to Grow

Water: Onions require even moisture. Cycles of wet and dry will cause the onion to produce several smaller bulbs instead of one big one. Increase watering as the bulb begins to form and swell. Decrease watering two weeks before harvesting.

Fertilizer: Incorporate compost or a balanced, slow-release fertilizer into the planting bed before planting onions. If you are growing onions in sandy soil, sidedress every four weeks during the growing season with a balanced fertilizer.

Pest control: Onion root maggots are the most problematic pests for onions. Good sanitation and removing dead plant leaves, will help control them.

When and How to Harvest

For bulbing onions, start the harvest process thirty days prior to the maturity date. Gradually pull the soil from the bulbs. After a month, bulbs should be ⅓ to ¾ uncovered, the leaves browning and falling over. Uproot them and lay them on top of the soil (leaves and all) to cure (dry) for two to five days. For storage, cut the tops off, leaving 1 inch of stalk to dry on the bulbs. You can store short-day onions for two to three months in a cool environment with low humidity.

Scallions can be harvested as needed, either the entire plant or just some leaves snipped off.

Harvest bunching onions when they are at least 2 inches in diameter. Pull up the entire plant, and chop it for use in salads, soups, stews, and sandwiches.

PEA *(Pisum sativum)*

One of my favorite vegetables is the edible pod pea, including snap and snow peas. Eat them right off the vine and they are so sweet and delicious! Shelling peas (remove them from the pod before eating) are also savory and pea shoots, the top 6 inches of the pea plant, are also edible (just ask the rabbits in my area). Cook pea shoots like you'd cook braising greens, or sauté them in olive oil and lemon juice with a bit of garlic and toss with pasta. Yum! Peas are another vegetable that will save you a lot of money if you grow your own. It's expensive to buy tasty fresh peas, but inexpensive to grow them.

■ *Recommended Varieties*

SHELLING PEAS: Heirloom 'Wando' is heat and cold resistant and ideal throughout the Southwest. Add 'Green Arrow' and 'Maestro' in the upper elevations. For shelling peas to dry and use in soups and stews consider these land races developed over the last 400 years by Southwestern substance farmers and available through Native Seeds: SEARCH: 'San Luis', 'Tarahumara Chicharos', and 'Truchas Alverjon'.

SNAP PEAS: Consider 'Sugar Ann', 'Sugar Snap', and pink-flowered 'Taichung'.

SNOW PEAS: 'Dwarf Grey' is a shorter plant that features purple and white flowers, a nice addition to the garden, also consider 'Oregon Giant' or 'Usui' with the traditional white flowers.

■ *When and Where to Plant*

Temperature: Soil temperature needs to be 60°F to 70°F. Snap peas especially, with the high sugar content, can easily rot in soils that are too cool. In cool upland gardens, you can bare the soil and lay down a nice dark-colored layer of seed starter mix to help warm the soil. But in desert gardens you may need to cool the soil—wet, then mulch the soil with straw or white swimming pool sand. Consider successive crops of peas, about a week apart. Then they'll ripen at different times and you won't be overwhelmed with more peas than you know what to do with.

Plant: Low and Middle Desert peas are for the winter garden, plant from September into mid-October. You can try planting again from mid-February into March and hope it doesn't get too hot too fast for a second crop. In the High Desert, plant your peas around April Fools Day. Cool Highlands, plant on May Day, and Cold Mountains plant on Memorial Day (for harvest on the Fourth of July). High Desert and Cool Plateau you can plant again in August, and if the frost holds off until its "official" day, you can enjoy a second crop of peas for the year; otherwise harvest and enjoy pea shoots.

Soil: Soil pH is ideally 6.0 to 7.0 and well-drained. Added compost is good but avoid adding steer manure or other fertilizer to soil before you plant peas, as it may actually retard their growth. If your garden has never been home to any legume plants, consider adding legume inoculant when you plant. This is the symbiotic bacteria the peas will need to make their own fertilizer.

Sun: Full sun.

Growing your own peas can save you money at the grocery store.

How to Plant

Starting seeds indoors: Not recommended.

Planting outside: Seeds need to be 1 inch deep. Space seeds 3 inches apart when planting. Seeds may take 14 days to emerge.

How to Grow

Water: Keep the soil evenly moist, but not soaking wet. Do not allow the soil to completely dry out.

Fertilizer: Avoid fertilizing peas. As legumes, the bacteria they live in harmony with take nitrogen out of the air and make fertilizer for the plants. Added fertilizer may actually stunt their growth. If your pea plants begin to yellow and appear as if they need nitrogen, what they really need is for the soil to be acidified. Sprinkle the soil with coffee grounds and water it in. The problem is alkaline-induced chlorosis, and is easy to solve.

Pest control: After quail, rabbits, javalina, and deer, aphids are the biggest pest problem for peas. Use insecticidal soap according to package instructions to control the pests.

When and How to Harvest

Peas will be ready for harvest forty-five to sixty days after planting. Pick or clip off individual pods carefully to avoid injury to the plant. Production can continue for weeks if the weather cooperates.

Harvest snap peas when the pods are plump but still dark green. Harvest snow peas when the pods are still relatively flat. Spent flowers might still be hanging on to the ends of the pods of both types of peas when you harvest these.

Harvest shelling peas when the pods are plump but still dark green. Once the pods start to turn yellow, the sugars in the peas convert to starch, and they aren't tasty anymore.

POTATO *(Solanum tuberosum)*

Say "potato" (or pahtato) and most folks think of Ireland. In fact, potatoes originated halfway around the world from the Emerald Isle. Not from Ireland where the average elevation is 400 feet, but from the Andean mountains, where 4,000 feet is the lowlands. Early Incan tribes learned that wild potatoes are a life-sustaining storehouse of energy and nutrients. They subsequently domesticated over 100 different varieties. These well-fed mountain people went on to found mighty empires, constructing extensive systems of roads, far-reaching irrigation canals, and vast cities.

Per unit of land, potatoes provide more protein and calories than any other food crop; five times more than soybeans, corn, or wheat. The tasty tubers also store a number of important vitamins and minerals found just below the skin (so you should always enjoy potatoes, skin and all).

With their origins in mind, you can understand that potatoes are a cool-season crop. They grow best in early spring and late fall when the days are warm and the nights are cool. Although the potato is a cool-season crop and the edible part of the plant is underground, the tops won't withstand frost. Timing is critical. You need to get them into the ground as early as possible to get a crop before either summer heat or winter cold kills the plants.

■ *Recommended Cultivars & Varieties*

Buy certified disease-free seed potatoes. Avoid planting potatoes from the supermarket because they can carry disease on their skins. Since potatoes are closely related to tomatoes, peppers, and eggplant, which can all cross-infect one another, this can be a real disaster.

Smaller, more quickly maturing potatoes are preferred in Low and Middle Desert. Consider 'Yukon Gold', 'All Red', or 'Red Gold'. In High Desert, add to this list 'Rose Gold', 'Katahdin', and the heirloom fingerlings such as 'Rose Finn Apple' and 'Russian Banana'. Cool Highlands can grow all the previous plus the large russets such as 'Butte' and 'Burbank'. Cold Mountains must select from those that mature in 100 days or less, thus consider the High Desert list.

Digging for potatoes is a great way for children to get involved in the garden.

◼ *When and Where to Plant*

Temperature: Soil needs to be 45°F to 65°F.

Plant: In Low Desert, plant in January. In Middle Desert plant in February into mid-March. In the High Desert, Cool Highlands, and Cold Mountains plant three weeks before the last frost date.

Soil: Potatoes do best in a loose, well-drained, acid soil, with a pH of 5.5 to 6.5. Add ample compost to the planting area to help acidify the soil.

Sun: Potatoes require at least six hours of full sun each day.

◼ *How to Plant*

Starting seeds indoors: Not recommended.

Planting outside: Cut "seed" potatoes that are larger than a chicken egg into pieces about 1 inch across. Each piece should have at least one "eye" (the bud where the stem will grow from), preferably two eyes. Egg-sized and smaller tubers can be planted whole. Once cut, seed potato pieces need to heal or "cure" for twenty-four to forty-eight hours before planting. Plant these sections 3 to 4 inches deep and 1 foot apart. As plants mature, "hill" the plants slowly over time with sand or straw mulch up to 1 foot deep. The tubers will form in this hill and be easier to dig.

◼ *How to Grow*

Water: For best yields, keep soil evenly damp, not wet. Allow some drying between waterings. Be sure to supply water during tuber formation, signaled by the appearance of blossoms.

Fertilizer: Potatoes need fertilizer in their early stage of growth, so mix compost into the soil or apply a slow-release fertilizer before planting. If you miss preplanting fertilizer, wait until sprouts have leafed out. Avoid using manure, which can increase the incidence of potato scab disease.

Pest control: Potato plants can take a large amount of insect damage and still yield tasty tubers. Colorado potato beetle will need to be eradicated with neem oil, pyrethrin spray, or pheremone traps once they appear. Fungus too can take a toll on your crop. Select disease-resistant varieties. If you get a blight, discard all diseased material. Do not feed diseased potatoes to livestock such as chickens or hogs if you use their manure.

◼ *When and How to Harvest*

As the "Days to Maturity" near, feel in the soil around the plants and harvest one or two potatoes from each plant, leaving any small ones still attached to the plant to grow larger. Harvest the main crop when the foliage dies back. Let the soil dry out then pull the plants or carefully dig with a blunt tool to expose your treasured tubers. Brush soil gently off the potatoes; do not wash them. Cure them in the dark at 55°F for two weeks before storing them in a cool (40°F) root cellar or refrigerator.

RADISH *(Raphanus sativus)*

Radishes taste dandy fresh out of the garden, but can become too sharp if stored too long—the reason store-bought just doesn't cut it. Roots are the most commonly eaten part of the radish, but the young tops, and young seed pods are edible, too. Fun to grow, radishes are fast to germinate and mature, plus you can get a succession of crops from one package of seeds. Indeed, it's a good idea to sow successive crops of radishes so that they mature a week or so apart. Nobody needs sixty radishes at once! Radishes are beneficial plants for the vegetable garden because mature leaves deter pests and, when allowed to flower, they attract pollinators.

■ *Recommended Varieties*

Radish varieties are near infinite. 'Cherry Belle' is a typical round, red-on-the-outside, white-on-the-inside variety that most people think of when they think "radish." Radishes also come with skins that are white, green, purple, yellow, and even black. As long as you plant them in cool, amended garden soils, all varieties do well in the Southwest.

If radishes in general are too sharp for you, consider the mild daikon radish (*Raphanus sativus* var. *longipinnatus*). Also called Japanese radish, this long, large white radish is originally from continental Asia and has a wide variety of culinary uses. The "Chinese radish" is the same species only generally rounder. There are also greener, rounder spicier varieties referred

Because radishes grow so quickly, they are a good plant for children to grow.

to as "Korean radish." Grow any of these as you would a typical radish, but note the longer "Days to Maturity" on the seed packet. Store these radishes in a cool dry place with the leaves removed. If left in the ground, they tend to become woody. Unless you have deep soil, select from these smaller varieties: 'Iwai Daikon', 'Karaine Hybrid', 'Shogoin Globe', or 'White Icicle'.

When and Where to Plant

Temperature: The soil temperature has to be between 45°F and 80°F for radishes to germinate.

Plant: In the Lower Desert, radishes can be planted starting October 1 and sown successively right through the winter. In Middle Desert, plant radishes after September 1 and until November 1. You can start planting again after February 15, and plan to harvest by April 15. In High Desert, plant in mid-March. In Cool Highlands and Cold Mountain, plant after last frost.

Soil: The books all say pH should be 6.0 to 7.0, but I have successfully grown radishes in desert soil (pH 8.2). This leads me to say that radishes are not overly picky about soil, but for good root formation, a lighter, sandy soil is recommended. Also, like any root crop, radishes will rot if the soil is slow-draining or stays too wet.

Sun: Full sun to light shade.

How to Plant

Starting seeds indoors: Not recommended.

Planting outside: Sow successive plantings of radish seeds outside as mentioned above. Plant seeds ½ inch deep and 1 to 2 inches apart.

How to Grow

Water: Radishes aren't fussy, but they do need even moisture levels to avoid cracking.

Fertilizer: Radishes do not need much fertilizer. To grow larger roots, you can fertilize with fish emulsion two weeks after planting.

Pest control: Fast growing and rarely bothered by pests, radishes may encounter flea beetles or aphids. Use row covers or spray with insecticidal soap.

When and How to Harvest

Don't let the radishes linger. They taste best when harvested after three to four weeks of growth, when they are still relatively small. The older the radishes, the more fibrous and stringy they get, and the more pungent the flavor becomes. They can be stored in the refrigerator or root cellar, tops removed, for two to four weeks.

TURNIP & RUTABAGA
(Brassica rapa var. *rapa)* and *(Brassica napobrassica)*

Turnips and their cousins the rutabaga are schizophrenic vegetables—in some regions they are grown for greens; in other areas the roots are the part relished. Either way, turnips and rutabaga are cool-weather vegetables. When you think of a turnip, you probably think of large, purple or white, globe-shaped roots, but there are other smaller, sweeter varieties, too. If you've never thought much about these chunky root crops, give them a try. They're naturally high in vitamin C, easy to grow, and taste great instead of potatoes in stews or with roast beef. For folks who medically avoid potatoes and other members of the deadly nightshade family, these roots are excellent alternatives.

■ *Recommended Varieties*

TURNIP: 'Golden Globe' is small and sweet. More traditional are 'Purple Top White Globe' and 'White Lady'. 'All Top' is grown specifically for turnip greens. 'Hakurei' is a small, white salad turnip that tastes good shredded raw into salads.

RUTABAGA: 'Joan' and 'American Purple Top' work well.

Turnips are grown both for their leafy green tops and their bulbous roots.

When and Where to Plant

Temperature: Turnip and rutabaga seeds will sprout when the weather is warm, but they need cool temperatures to mature if you want to harvest sweet roots.

Plant: Sow seeds directly in fall for the winter garden in Low and Middle Desert. Sow right after last frost in the Cold Mountains. In High Desert and Cool Highlands, sow in July in the area you just harvested your onions or garlic from. If planting for greens or small roots for salad, consider successive plantings, like for radish.

Soil: Rich, well-drained, acidic soil with pH 6.4 to 7.2.

Sun: Full sun.

How to Plant

Starting seeds indoors: As with all root crops, not recommended.

Planting outside: Sow seeds two seeds per inch, ¼ to ½ inch deep. In the winter garden, cover with light-colored sand to help keep cool. In upper elevations, cover with a seed-starting mix to encourage germination. Thin turnips to 6 inches apart for growing. Don't forget to throw the thinnings into the salad bowl. Rutabaga grows to larger size, and thus spacing needs to be 8 inches apart.

How to Grow

Water: Keep the soil evenly moist but not soggy. Straw mulch can help with this.

Fertilizer: Add compost to the bed before planting and fertilize with a well-balanced fertilizer once every four weeks or so after planting in any frost-free month.

Pest control: The biggest concern with turnips is to avoid planting them in exactly the same place that you grew any cole crops (*Brassicas*) in the previous year. Pesky aphids can be controlled with insecticidal soap. Control flea beetles by using floating row covers.

When and How to Harvest

How you harvest depends on which part of the plant you wish to harvest. Young, tender greens can be harvested when they are 2 to 4 inches tall. Young, tender roots, 2 inches in diameter, can be used raw in salads. When roots reach 3 or 4 inches in diameter, they're ready to be pulled up and used for roasting, mashing or pickling. Turnip roots are sweeter in flavor when they go through a frost.

Rutabaga is generally better for long-term storage. With the larger size, rutabaga needs to stay in the ground three to six weeks longer than turnips, but it is more cold-tolerant and can take light freezes in the autumn, developing a sweeter flavor.

A selection of cool-season herbs cut for use as garnishes.

Cool-Season Herbs

In the Southwest, the cool-season herbs are mainly in the carrot family. This means that their care is highly similar—but not exactly the same—which is why gardening is both an art and a science. Once you have grown the cool-season carrot family members discussed in this chapter, you may wish to try other members of the family as well, such as angelica, anise, asafoetida, chervil, cicely, cumin, fennel, or lovage.

Cool-season herbs that are not in the carrot family are numerous. I do hope you will try some. Think herbs from northern Europe or northern North America in general. German chamomile prefers cool climates, while the Roman chamomile (a different species) is a warm-season herb.

Echinacea, native to the prairies of North America, does not like the extensive heat of Desert Zone gardens, but can be grown in the two Upper Zones. Bergamot, also called bee balm, can be grown in the Cool Plateau and Cold Mountains in summer. Do you see the trend? I wish I could include more of these wonderful plants, but I wanted this book to apply to as many readers as possible.

Harvesting Herb Seed

The seed of three of these four cool-season herbs are commonly found in cooking—caraway, coriander, and dill. To harvest your plants for the seed, uproot the entire plant once it begins to yellow and die. If you leave the plants in the garden until they are entirely brown, the birds will get the seed, plus they will scatter seed all over your garden. Uproot your plant and turn it upside down in a large paper bag or cardboard box and let the seed dry completely; this can be two to three weeks. Once dry, crumble the seed off the plant. Clean the seed by shaking it in a large kitchen strainer to let the leafy bits fall through and keep the seed in the strainer. Use your herb seeds in cooking within a year or two before their strong flavorful oils degrade.

Italian parsley

CILANTRO/CORIANDER & PARSLEY
(Coriandrum sativum) and *(Petroselinum crispum)*

Cilantro and parsley share virtually identical care, and have many of the same uses, thus they are together here. Most of us Southwesterners think of salsa when we hear cilantro, but it has historic use as a digestive aid, much like parsley (which is why it used to grace plates in restaurants). While cilantro can get along with the heat of chilies in salsa, it and cousin parsley both quickly bolt and then die with the heat of a standard summer day. Therefore you will want to grow these herbs in the cool months.

Hate the taste of cilantro? You are not alone. Scientists agree that there appears to be a genetic component to cilantro taste preference. Those that like the herb find it pungent and tangy, those that don't often say it tastes soapy. It's your genes, and both experiences are equally valid. Incidentally, it is not just Mexican recipes that call for cilantro/coriander, so do many Asian dishes, but it is less evident as a flavor in Asian cooking where it is often hidden by the flavors of curry and other ingredients.

Both parsley and coriander could be justified as a garden plant if only for the job they do in attracting bees and other pollinators to the garden. Coriander honey is prized for its flavor. I let both parsley and cilantro produce flowers and go to seed so I have coriander seed. I leave the parsley seed in the garden for the lesser goldfinch to enjoy. Since these charming birds also eat insect pests, inviting them into my garden helps us both.

■ *Recommended Varieties*

Due to our long, comparatively warm days, even during our "cool" season, you need to select varieties that are slow to bolt.

CILANTRO: 'Long Standing', 'Sabor', 'Slo-Bolt'.
PARSLEY: Curled-leaf parsleys are preferred for eating. Good varieties for our region are: 'Moss Curled', 'Sweet Curly', and 'Triple Curled'. Italian parsley is considered better for cooking and drying due to stronger flavor. 'Italian Dark' and 'Italian Giant' have both done well in my garden.

■ *When and Where to Plant*

Temperature: Seeds will germinate with soil temperatures of 50°F to 70°F. While the plants like to grow during cool weather, they are frost sensitive.
Soil: Requires rich, well-drained, loose soil, pH 6.2 to 7.2. Containers are fine but must be 18 inches or greater in depth.
Sun: Six or more hours of sun per day.

144

■ *How to Plant*

Cilantro

Starting seeds indoors: Of all the carrot family members, these two are the most likely to tolerate transplanting. They are also very easy to find as seedlings in nurseries. If you have ample indoor space you can start these indoors four to six weeks before transplanting outdoors.

Planting outside: Two or three plants are usually enough for most families so seedlings might be a better option. Otherwise, sow seeds ¼ inch deep and thickly, three or four seeds per inch. Cover with seed-starting mix. Keep the seeds evenly moist for the time it takes to germinate, often up to two weeks. Use scissors to thin to one plant every 12 inches. You can use the thinnings in salads.

Curly parsley

■ *How to Grow*

Water: All members of the carrot family prefer to be kept in evenly moist soil.

Fertilizer: For best flavor and flowering (for seed) fertilize with a balanced fertilizer two weeks after germination, and once per month in any non-freezing month.

Pest control: These herbs are susceptible to the same pests found on carrots and parsnips. Keep an eye out for aphids and flea beetles and treat with insecticidal soap.

■ *When and How to Harvest*

Select tender young leaves and snip off with scissors. Try not to take more than half the plant at once so it has enough energy to regrow. Both cilantro and parsley leaves taste great when fresh but lose flavor when dried. Freezing the leaves retains more flavor. Select healthy leaves, rinse, pat dry but leave some moisture. Chop into roughly ¼-inch squares and freeze in a labeled plastic bag or yogurt container. This can be used directly from the freezer. See page 143 for seed harvest and storage information.

Dill leaves can be used in salads and the seeds in flavoring.

DILL & CARAWAY
(Anethum graveolens) and *(Carum carvi)*

Dill and caraway are members of the carrot family, and have highly similar care requirements, but usage differs. Dill leaves offer a spritely tang to fresh garden salads and perks up frozen vegetables. Caraway leaves are used sometimes in the same way that parsley is. Both caraway and dill "seed" (technically a fruit) are used in a vast number of dishes, dill more for pickling while caraway is popular in baking and cheeses.

Both dill and caraway plants look just plain pretty in a garden, offering delicate, lacy foliage, and crowned heads late in the season with masses of tiny, warm yellow flowers borne in clusters called umbles (think upside down umbrella). These carrot family members are larval host plants for a number of butterfly species, including the two-tailed swallowtail, the Official Butterfly of the State of Arizona. This means you should plant some extra plants and tolerate caterpillars feeding on the plants. They emerge from their chrysalis later to pollinate the flowers. Indeed, the flowers are a nectar source for a number of beneficial insects and pollinators.

■ Recommended Varieties

Growing in the cool garden, heat tolerance is not so critical. Still, I have found that the plants that are genetically programmed to be smaller in size tend to do better than the mammoth varieties.

CARAWAY: Generally simply offered by name.
DILL: 'Bouquet', 'Dukat', 'Fernleaf', 'Swain Heirloom', 'Tetra'.

■ When and Where to Plant

Temperature: Seeds will germinate with soil temperatures of 50°F to 70°F. While the plant likes to grow during cool weather, it is frost sensitive.
Soil: Requires rich, well-drained, loose soil, pH 6.5 to 7.5. Containers are fine but must be 18 inches or greater in depth.
Sun: Full sun.

■ How to Plant

Starting seeds indoors: Not recommended. These members of the carrot family have a taproot, which makes them difficult to transplant.
Planting outside: Sow seeds ¼ inch deep and thickly, three or four seeds per inch. Cover with seed-starting mix. Keep the seeds evenly moist for the time it takes to germinate, often up to two weeks. Use scissors to thin to one plant every 12 inches. You can use the thinnings in salads.

■ How to Grow

Water: All members of the carrot family prefer to be kept in evenly moist soil.
Fertilizer: For best flavor and flowering (for seed) fertilize with a balanced fertilizer two weeks after germination, and once per month in any nonfreezing month.
Pest control: These herbs are susceptible to the same pests found on carrots and parsnips. Keep an eye out for aphids and flea beetles and treat with insecticidal soap.

■ When and How to Harvest

The leaves are most fragrant and delicious before the plants start to flower. For fresh leaves, use kitchen scissors to snip off the tender younger leaves. Dill leaves may be dried for future use. Larger leaves can be used for this since they will be crumbled at use. Dry leaves out of direct sunlight and use within eighteen months before the flavorful oils decay. See the start of this section on cool-season herbs for seed harvest and storage.

A row of pollinator plants near the vegetable gardens help entice pollinators into the area.

Warm-Season Gardening Tips & Tricks

Almost all of the vegetables and herbs profiled in this section have tropical or subtropical ancestors, and need warmth to survive. Several crops were originally from the Southwest, notably chili peppers, originating in the mountains south of Tucson, Arizona.

Most of the warm-season "vegetables" are technically fruits—they have seeds inside. Some of these vegetables taste better before the seeds develop, like okra or zucchini. Others are entirely unpalatable if they are not ripe and ready to spread their seeds, like melon or peppers.

With these facts in mind, realize that your warm-season plants will need warm soil to grow in, plus ample time to develop into an edible crop. It is always tempting to try to get your corn in the ground "nice and early," but it can be a deadly mistake—for the corn seeds that is. They easily rot in cold soils. Plant profiles provide guidelines and desired soil temperatures, almost all at 65°F or greater.

Water in the Warm Season

Water will be required if you opt to garden in the warm-season. Soaker hoses and driplines discussed in Chapter 4 will help the process, but do not rely entirely on electronic gizmos to control these water delivery systems. You need to check your garden daily because batteries fail, pipes leak, and power bumps are common in summer storms.

Plan on a good layer of mulch for the garden—the difference in water use is astounding. Also plan on watering deeply to encourage deep roots. Except for the warm-season greens, everything in this section easily roots to 18 inches or more. If you water sufficiently so the moisture is 18 inches deep, it will not evaporate as quickly, and you may only need to water every third day—even in 100-degree heat. This can result in significant savings on your water bill.

Pollination Required

As mentioned above, most of these warm-season vegetables are in reality the fruit of the plant. The flowers must be pollinated before the fruit can develop. Help is needed for this, wind in the case of corn, but all the rest are insect pollinated. Failing insects and wind, you will need to do the pollination yourself, a tedious task.

To better your chance of insects taking care of pollination in the garden, plant insect-attracting plants. While it is ideal to place pollinator attractors right in the garden, for most of my readers with raised beds the space is simply not available. This is where you turn to the landscape around your garden. Consider planting the perennial herbs listed in the Warm-Season Herbs section (page 186). Both aloysia and basil attract pollinators with blooms that

Okra can be grown for its beautiful flowers as well as vegetables.

Planting a wide variety of vegetables, herbs, and flowers together confuses pests.

continue right through the warm season. You can also leave some cool-season plants to flower and seed, like radish, arugula, and the cool-season herbs. Consider adding pollinator plants throughout the rest of your landscape—flowering perennials that do well in your zone such as lantana, verbena, or salvia.

Dealing with Pests

"Summer time, and the living is easy." That's the song summer pests are singing as they munch away on your garden. There are different remedies for different pests. In the warm-season garden, floating row covers are often recommended, a better option than spraying. But better yet, consider these two options.

Option 1: Plant a variety of plants in clustered groupings in various areas. If there is not a massive amount of the plant in any one location, it makes it harder for the mother "bug" to simply find the right plant to lay her eggs on. The closer you mimic nature, the closer your garden is to a natural ecosystem, the more beneficial insects you will attract to it.

Option 2: Reconsider what you think "pest damage" is. Plants themselves have been living with pests for eons and holes in leaves are not a big deal to them. Corn ear worms? Yuck if you squish one unexpectedly, but I go around with tweezers, yank them out of the ears, and drop them in soapy water. When it comes time to cook the corn, I rinse off the frass (droppings) and chop off the damaged section.

ONE BIG PROBLEM IN THE SOUTHWEST—BLOSSOM-END ROT

"Blossom-end rot" refers to a rotten-looking area on the end of a fruiting vegetable which appears where the blossom once was. It is a cultural problem, caused by the gardener's care, not a true rot-caused mold or fungus. In the Southwest, the problem occurs most commonly when watering is inconsistent. Use drippers or soaker hoses to help ensure even watering and mulch the soil well to help avoid this problem. Selecting small-fruited varieties will also help avoid the problem. Finally, although it is not a caused by a fungus, the cavity that appears with blossom-end rot can easily get moldy if water gets in there and sits.

AMARANTH (*Amaranthus* species)

Amaranth flowers will attract hummingbirds to your garden.

Amaranth is both a grain and a green. Young tender leaves can be used anywhere you would use spinach, raw or cooked. At the end of the season, the plants produce massive heads full of tasty, quick cooking, nutritious grain—gluten-free grain!

There are over sixty species of amaranth around the world, and while several species are considered weeds, many people around the world value amaranths as vegetables, for the seeds, for dye, and as ornamental plants. Some species of amaranth, although eaten as "greens" are anything but green in color. Foliage ranges in hue from crimson, to red, to vivid magenta, all due to natural pigments called betalains. Whatever their color, they are a good source of vitamins A, B_3, B_6, C, and K, and folate, along with dietary minerals calcium, iron, magnesium, phosphorus, potassium, zinc, copper, and especially manganese.

Amaranth seeds, like the seeds of quinoa and buckwheat, contain what are commonly called "complete protein" (a complete set of the amino acids needed by humans). These three are called "pseudograins" because of their flavor and cooking similarities to grains, but unlike grain, they do not contain gluten. Amaranth grows very rapidly and its large seedheads can weigh several pounds and contain a half-million seeds. These seeds can be boiled, parched, or even toasted much like popcorn and mixed with honey, molasses, or chocolate to make a Mexican treat called *alegría*. You may have already grown amaranth, because the genus also contains well-known ornamental plants, such as love-lies-bleeding (*Amaranthus caudatus*), prince's feather (*Amaranthus hypochondriacus*), and Joseph's coat (*Amaranthus tricolor*).

■ *Recommended Cultivars & Varieties*

Low Desert: 'Alamos', 'Guarijio Grain', 'Kerala Red', 'Mayo Grain', 'Red Garnet', 'Red Leaf'.

Middle Desert: 'Alamos', 'Golden Grain', 'Guarijio Grain', 'Mayo Grain', 'Red Garnet', 'Red Leaf'.

High Desert: 'Alamos', 'Golden Grain', 'Guarijio Grain', 'Hopi Red Dye', 'Red Beauty'.

Cool Highlands: 'Elephant Head', 'Hopi Red Dye', 'Red Beauty'.

Cold Mountain: 'Elephant Head', 'Hopi Red Dye', 'Polish', 'Red Beauty'.

When and Where to Plant

Temperature: Soils should warm and the chance of frost should be past.

Soil: If you plant Southwestern cultivars, pH can be as high as 8.0, otherwise 6.0 to 7.0.

Sun: Full sun for at least six hours a day. Afternoon shade in Desert zones is okay.

How to Plant

Starting seeds indoors: Not recommended.

Planting outside: Plant in spring or with the summer rains by broadcasting and raking in tiny seeds. Alternatively plant ¼ inch deep in basins or in rows. Thin the edible seedlings to 10 to 15 inches apart, adding the thinnings to salads.

How to Grow

Water: Keep young seedlings moist, but as plants mature allow the soil to dry somewhat between watering.

Fertilizer: Not required, although high phosphorous, fruiting or flowering fertilizer when plants begin to flower will ensure good seed production.

Pest control: Few pests bother amaranth to excess. In fact, amaranth is a beneficial plant in the garden, serving as a trap for leaf miners and some other pests, as well as sheltering Southwestern ground beetles (which prey upon insect pests) plus breaking up hard soil for more delicate neighboring plants.

When and How to Harvest

Young amaranth leaves are tasty right off the plant, in salads, or steamed as a potherb. In Greece, the native green amaranth (*Amaranthus viridis*) is used in a popular dish called *vleeta*, consisting of boiled leaves served with olive oil and lemon.

Mature seedheads of amaranth are harvested while still somewhat green, before the bracts open to release the seed. Harvest early so the seed will drop when and where you can more easily capture it, like within a paper bag or onto a clean sheet. Also, if you handle the material carefully, you can reduce the need for winnowing. Amaranth seed can be cooked for a high-protein pseudograin or ground into a flour or meal for baking. As with rice and other grains, use two cups liquid to one cup grain.

BEANS

Bean categories are confusing. Beans can be divided by growth habit (climbing, pole, semi-pole, bush) or stage of growth when eaten (snap or green, shell, dry). Some beans aren't even called beans—and yet they are, like the black-eyed pea, eaten as either a shell or dry bean. Some people can eat some species of beans but have violent food allergies to other species, kidney and soy being two problematic species. Beans are primarily a warm-weather crop and can do quite well in our high heat and low humidity. My personal favorite is the Southwest native tepary bean (cultivated here for more than 4,000 years). A dry bean, the tepary is otherwise very "green" since it grows well in straight desert soil, grows quickly with little extra water, and cooks quickly, too. The "green" tepary bean saves garden space for other vegetables, the cost of using water, and the energy to cook it. One further plus, tepary is the highest in protein and lowest in carbohydrates of all the dry beans.

Green beans (bush and otherwise) and fava beans are the exception to the warm-weather rule, preferring cooler times for growing. In Low and Middle Desert plant these last two types in autumn to harvest in spring, and in the upper zones plant in early spring for harvest in early summer.

■ *Recommended Varieties*

When possible, select Bean Common Mosaic Virus (BCMV) resistant varieties.

BLACK-EYED PEA AND LONG BEAN (*Vigna unguiculata*): Desert Zones, 'Heirloom California Wonder', 'Red Noodle', and 'Tohono O'odham Heirloom' are good to grow, but for the Upper Zones, 'Coronet Pinkeye Purple Hull', 'Midori Giant', and 'Queen Ann' are better as they mature more quickly.

FAVA (*Vicia faba*): 'Heirloom Windsor', 'Moonlight', and 'Scarlet Emperor' all work in the Southwest.

GARBANZO (*Cicer arietinum*): Available in some catalogs, but no specific cultivars (yet).

GREEN BEAN OR POLE BEAN (*Phaseolus vulgaris*): Can be yellow when ripe. Decide if you want bush or pole. Good producers in marginally alkaline soils like ours are 'Blue Lake', 'Gold Rush', and 'Pencil Pod.'

LIMA (*Phaseolus lunatus*): Desert gardens, select from 'Pima Beige', 'Pima Orange.' Upper elevations select from 'Calico', 'Hopi Gray', 'Hopi Red', 'Hopi Yellow'.

Pole beans growing up a trellis

RUNNER (*Phaseolus coccineus*): Not ideal for the heat of Middle and Low Desert. Upper Desert and above, select from 'Aztec White', 'Scarlet', or 'Tarahumara Bordal.'

TEPARY (*Phaseolus acutifolius*): Desert zones: 'Big Fields', 'Black', 'Brown Speckled', 'Cocopah Brown', 'Pinacate', and 'Tohono O'odham White' do well. Upper elevations, 'Blue Speckled' produces wonderfully.

■ *When and Where to Plant*

Temperature: Soil temperature should be at least 60°F before planting beans.

Soil: Soil pH should be between 6.5 and 7.5 for most bean species. Tepary beans tolerate desert soils with a pH of 8.0 to 8.5.

Sun: Full sun to light shade. Teparies and pole beans are one of the Three Sisters. If you use a trellis for your climbing beans, select an area on the north side of the garden so that they won't shade out the rest of your plants.

■ *How to Plant*

Starting seeds indoors: Not recommended or needed.

Planting outside: Planting depth depends on the bean species—in general plant it twice as deep as it is long. Thus a large lima bean goes into 1-inch-deep hole while tiny tepary beans are planted only ¼ to ½ inch deep. Beans can also be seeded in mounds or hills with corn and squash, four or five seeds to a hill. Or you can omit the corn and put a trellis or tomato cage over each hill.

■ *How to Grow*

Water: Beans are somewhat drought-tolerant until they start flowering. Once plants start flowering, the beans should be kept evenly moist.

Fertilizer: Beans work with nitrogen-fixing bacteria to get all the nitrogen they need out of the soil. Thus if you give them a high-nitrogen fertilizer you can actually stunt their growth. Avoid planting marigolds near beans or peas, since marigold roots contain bacteria-killing compounds. You can purchase bean inoculant to place in the soil as you plant beans, but it is not required if you have gardened in the area before.

Pest control: Pest problems include stinkbugs, Mexican bean beetles, Japanese beetles, junebugs, thrips, and aphids. Row covers can keep stinkbugs and beetles away from plants. Use insecticidal soap to control thrips and aphids.

■ *When and How to Harvest*

For green beans, it's time to harvest once pods start forming—while pods are still tender. Beans should easily break in half and be easy to snap off the plant when they're ready to harvest. To keep plants producing, pick regularly. If beans are allowed to yellow on the plant, the plant will stop producing.

To harvest shelling beans such as limas, garbanzos, and black-eyed peas, wait until the pods start bulging and then pick.

To harvest dry beans, allow the pods to begin to dry on the plant. Some varieties will continue to produce if you pluck these ripe pods. At the end of the season, pull up the entire plant and dry it on a clean bedsheet. Thresh the pods and collect the beans. Seal away from insect pests (canning jars work well) in a cool, dark area. Use the beans within the year for best nutrition and flavor.

CORN (MAIZE) *(Zea mays* varieties*)*

Corn is a wind-pollinated plant, so you have to grow the plants close together in blocks so the wind can blow the pollen from plant to plant.

In Europe, "corn" is the generic term for any grain. Here in North America we use the name for the native crop that has been grown in our Southwestern backyard for more than 4,000 years (Bat Cave, New Mexico, and Tucson, Arizona, oldest sites in the United States). Corn has been cultivated in Mesoamerica since 6700 B.C.E., and since its discovery, corn has been bred for a variety of uses depending on starch versus sugar content and moisture levels. Now we have sweet corn, popcorn, plus dent, flint, and flour corn for grinding into flour, parching, feeding to livestock, and making biofuels. Gardens of all sizes can grow at least a few ears of corn. The secret is to tightly cluster your corn so it can be pollinated. Since corn is wind pollinated and the pollen grains are relatively huge, plant your corn in blocks or clusters, not rows. I help my corn get pollinated by shaking the tassels on the top of the stalks once I see the yellow pollen forming. Corn requires ample water and nitrogen, and natives dealt with these issues by planting the "Three Sisters," together in dense clusters: corn, beans, and squash. Corn provides the pole for the beans to climb, the beans fix the nitrogen for the corn to use, and the squash shades the soil to reduce evaporation.

■ *Recommended Varieties, based on use*

GRINDING AND PARCHING CORN (Dent corn, *Zea mays* var. *indentata*, Flint corn, *Zea mays* var. *indurata*, and Flour corn, *Zea mays* var. *amylacea*): In Desert gardens try 'Tohono O'odham', Upper Zones 'Hopi Blue Sakwapu', or 'Hopi Wekte.' If you wish to try the ancient method of parching to preserve corn as a "trail mix," 'Santo Domingo' is a good choice.

POPCORN (*Zea mays* var. *everta*): Desert Zones consider 'Chapalote Pinole Maiz', or 'Cochiti.' Upper Elevations, the 'Tarahumara' can also be used for flour. Everybody should try the 'Glass Gem', just because it is beautiful.

SWEET CORN (*Zea mays* var. *saccharata* and *Zea mays* var. *rugosa*): Low Desert, 'Maricopa' or 'Yuman Yellow.' Middle Desert, 'Golden Bantam' and 'Golden Bantam.' High Desert, 'Mountain Pima Yellow' or 'Golden Bantam.' Cool Highlands and Cold Mountains, 'Hopi Sweet Tawaktchi' or 'Paiute.'

▤ *When and Where to Plant*

Temperature: Corn does not grow well in cold soil. Wait to plant until soil temperatures are above 70°F. In the upper zones, you can plant and cover seed with dark seed-starter mix.

Soil: Add an ample compost to help bring the soil pH to 6.0 to 7.0. The Southwestern Heirloom varieties can grow in soil with pH of 7.0 to 8.0.

Sun: Full sun to light afternoon shade in Low and Middle Desert locations.

▤ *How to Plant*

Starting seeds indoors: Not recommended or needed.

Planting outside: Once soil is warm, plant in blocks, not rows. Corn plants get big but don't mind crowding—which helps maintain humidity. Seeds can be planted 6 inches apart in rows 18 inches apart if you have room. If you are growing corn in a small space, make sure to plant at least twelve stalks spaced 8 inches apart, in a square.

▤ *How to Grow*

Water: Corn requires consistent moisture through the growing season— more moisture when it starts to tassel (flower). Plant the Three Sisters or mulch the soil with straw to reduce evaporation.

Fertilizer: Corn requires a great deal of nitrogen. Prepare area by adding compost and a slow-release fertilizer before planting. If you do not plant the "Three Sisters," then add a high-nitrogen fertilizer once a month in the growing season.

Pest control: There are many pests that attack corn plants. Corn earworm (a moth caterpillar) is perhaps the most disheartening because the main treatment is *Bacillus thuringiensis* (*B.t.*), a product lethal to all butterflies and moths. Treat only as needed if you have an infestation. Raccoons and birds also adore corn. To deter raccoons, play a radio (talk shows are good) or put in an electric fence. Birds are scared off with scarecrows with long fluttery clothing. Old CDs swirling on thin string also work.

▤ *When and How to Harvest*

Sweet corn is ready to harvest when milky-white juice squirts from a kernel pierced by a fingernail. Start checking after the silks start to turn brown. To harvest, hold the corn stalk in one hand and grasp the ripe ear with the other hand, then pull downward and twist the ear, and you won't yank the plant out of the ground.

Dry corn is ready to harvest when the plant starts to turn brown and die. Take the ears, remove the husks, and cure the cobs for an additional four to six weeks (on a screen if you can). Once cured, take the kernels off the cobs and store in sealed containers. Use within the year.

CUCUMBER *(Cucumis sativus)*

Cucumbers are members of the squash family, also called the "cucurbits." Just like the cabbage family includes many related cold-season vegetables, the cucurbits include many related warm-season vegetables. This presents a double challenge. Once cucurbit pests find your garden, it is difficult to control them. Second, if you plan to save seed, you can't allow your plants to cross-pollinate or the seed you save for next year will result in inedible vegetables. I simply purchase new cucurbit seed each year from folks whose job it is to provide pure strains. One of the worst pests in the Southwest is the squash vine borer, but is also the easiest to treat, so plant away and enjoy these savory cucumbers and other members of the squash family!

■ Recommended Varieties

Cucumber seeds are listed in catalogs with resistance to some of the most prevalent cucumber diseases. CMV refers to cucumber mosaic virus, which can be a problem. DM means resistant to downy mildew, and PM means resistant to powdery mildew. Both of these mildews are seldom a problem unless we have extensive monsoon rains. When in doubt, play it safe by selecting resistant varieties. To avoid blossom-end rot problems, select from smaller sized varieties.

GARDEN OR SLICING:
Low Desert: 'Lemon', 'Marketmore', 'Poona Kheera', 'Suyo Long', 'Yamoto'.
Middle and High Desert: 'Lemon', 'Marketmore', 'Poinsett', 'Straight Eights', 'Yamoto'.
Cool and Cold elevations: 'Lemon', 'Marketmore', 'Spacemaster', 'White Wonder'.

PICKLING:
Low Desert: 'Arkansas Little Leaf', 'Lemon'.
Middle and High Desert: 'Arkansas Little Leaf', 'Lemon', 'SMR 58'.
Cool and Cold elevations: 'Boston Pickling', 'Edmonson', 'Lemon', 'Richmond Green Apple', 'White Wonder'.

■ When and Where to Plant

Temperature: Plant after danger of frost has passed and the soil is 60°F to 70°F.
Soil: Cucumbers grow best in soils with a pH of 6.0 to 7.0. They require ample water, at the same time they require well-draining soil. Add plenty of compost to the soil before planting.
Sun: Full sun to light afternoon shade in desert gardens.

■ *How to Plant*

Starting seeds indoors: Not recommended; squash family members do not transplant well. That said, in the Cold Mountains, start three weeks before last frost in biodegradable pots.

Planting outside: Sow seeds ½ inch deep. Plant in mounds or rows with 8 to 12 inches between plants.

Growing cucumbers up a trellis saves space in the garden.

■ *How to Grow*

Water: Keep the soil evenly moist during the entire growing period, but especially once they begin to flower and produce fruit. Place drip tubes or soaker hoses along the base of cucumber plants to help deliver a steady stream of water at the roots. Mulch uncovered soil around plants.

Fertilizer: Cucumbers need high levels of phosphorous and potassium for good production. Sidedress cucumbers every two weeks during the growing season with a balanced fertilizer.

Pest control: Cucumber beetles and squash vine borers are the peskiest pests to attack cucumbers. Select narrow-stemmed varieties (listed), or protect large stems with petroleum jelly or aluminum foil. You can also place floating row covers over young plants and remove the covers when the plants flower. Neem oil and pyrethrum are two organic pesticides that can help control the pests.

■ *When and How to Harvest*

Once cucumber fruits start forming, keep your eyes peeled for any fruits that need to be picked. You can't let cucumbers sit on the vine, because they will develop a bitter taste. Worse yet, unpicked cucumbers will give the plant the message to stop producing any more fruit.

Seed package will indicate harvest size. In general harvest pickling cucumbers when they are 2 to 6 inches long. Harvest lemon cucumbers at 2 to 3 inches in diameter. Harvest slicing cucumbers when they are 6 to 12 inches long. Use your garden shears or pruners to cut the fruits off the vine. To minimize post-harvest water loss, leave roughly 1 inch of stem on the end of the fruit.

EGGPLANT *(Solanum melongena)*

Eggplants, along with tomatoes, peppers, chilies, potatoes, and tomatillos, are all members of the Solanaceae, or deadly nightshade, family. Some people simply can't eat any members of the family, and if you are one of these, console yourself with the fact that many of these use too much water to be good Southwestern garden plants. Nightshade vegetables are tropical in origin, and do relatively well here in the Southwest, but our sun can be too much of a good thing for these equatorial plants. Afternoon shade is the key to success with eggplant. At a loss for what to do with eggplants? Avoid heating the kitchen and try grilled eggplant (slice, salt, rinse, then brush with olive oil and grill). I use the slow cooker to make ratatouille (eggplant, onions, squash, and tomatoes) or caponata (eggplant, squash, onions, olives, and capers).

■ *Recommended Varieties*

Blossom-end rot is an issue with larger varieties, so select smaller varieties. Select the lighter skinned green or striped varieties to avoid sunscald.

Low Desert: 'Lao Purple Stripe', 'Rosita', 'White Beauty'.
Middle Desert: 'Early Black Egg', 'Lao Green Stripe', 'Listada de Gandi', 'Rosa Bianca', 'White Beauty'.
High Desert: 'Blush', 'Early Black Egg', 'Japanese White Egg', 'Korean Red', 'Rosa Bianca', 'Turkish Italian Orange'.
Cool Highlands: 'Blush', 'Early Black Egg', 'Japanese White Egg', 'Korean Red', 'Turkish Italian Orange'.
Cold Mountains: 'Applegreen', 'Early Black Egg', 'Thai Green', 'Turkish Italian Orange'.

■ *When and Where to Plant*

Temperature: Eggplants need soil and nighttime air temperatures to be at least 65°F and up to 85°F.
Soil: The pH should be 6.0 to 7.0 for best growth. Add compost to the soil before planting, and plant in well-drained locations.
Sun: Full sun in upper elevations, partial to afternoon shade in Desert gardens.

■ *How to Plant*

Starting seeds indoors: Start seeds indoors six to eight weeks before you want to plant outside.
Planting outside: Plant seeds ¼ inch deep. In Low and Middle Desert you can direct sow in spring once soil is warm enough, in the other

elevations, transplants are recommended. Depending on the mature size of the plant, plant seeds or transplants in staggered rows roughly 8 to 16 inches apart. Block planting helps conserve a humid area around the plants.

■ How to Grow

Water: Eggplants need a large, consistent supply of water. Use drippers or soaker hoses and mulch soil around plants for the best result.

Fertilizer: Eggplant needs ample phosphorous, and thus does best with a balanced fertilizer every two weeks during the growing season.

Pest control: Many pests and diseases call eggplants home. Colorado potato beetles, tomato hornworms, and flea beetles are the worst insect offenders. Keep plants under row covers until they have three sets of leaves to avoid problems with flea beetles. Keep an eye out for tomato hornworms, pick them off and drop them into a pail of soapy water (I use large cactus forceps to handle them). Look for the orange eggs of the Colorado potato beetle on the undersides of the leaves, and wash the leaves with water or crush the eggs to control them.

Eggplants come in different shapes and sizes. Look at your seed packet to find out what they're supposed to look like when ripe so you know when to harvest.

■ When and How to Harvest

Check the seed packet or plant label for when to harvest. It really depends on the variety you plant since some eggplant varieties are ripe at 3 inches and others get to be 8 inches or more. Ripe eggplants have shiny skin. If the skin is dull, they're past their prime, and you should pick them and throw them in the worm bin or compost heap. Use your scissors, pruners or a knife to cut the fruit, leaving around ½ inch of stem. Like all other warm-season crops, if you leave the fruits on the plant too long, they develop mature seeds and become bitter tasting.

GREENS, WARM-SEASON

Ceylon spinach

Just because it is 100°F doesn't mean you can't have a tasty, home-grown green salad. Well, it won't have lettuce in it, because lettuce is a cool-season crop. Instead, you will have to cultivate a suite of greens long used by local Natives, or new to us from other hot climates around the world. Some of these are better as cooked greens, in stir-fry or as a potherb. Not sure you want to devote a great deal of space to a crop you may not enjoy? These greens have shallow roots and can be grown in containers. Indeed, some are best grown in containers in a pond or water garden, with the bottom inch of the pot submerged and providing ample water for thirsty rainforest plants. Many have "spinach" in their common name, but most are not even in the same plant family as European spinach.

■ *Recommended Varieties*

CEYLON OR INDIA SPINACH (*Basella alba*): Does best with higher humidity levels, ideal in a water garden.

MALABAR SPINACH (*Basella alba* var. *rubra*): Asian vegetable that requires a trellis. In the Low and Middle Desert, plant on your pea trellises once peas are done for the winter. They may become perennial in a frost-free year.

MINERS SPINACH (*Atriplex hortensis* and *A. wrightii*): Often volunteers as a weed. Be sure you harvest it all before it goes to seed.

NEW ZEALAND SPINACH (*Tetragonia expansa*): Related to the flowering iceplant; eat it before it flowers. Commonly available in Southern seed catalogs.

PERILLA, SHISO (*Perilla frutescens*): Popular in East Asia as a potherb and in sushi, this mint family member is good in a water garden. Available in purple- and green-leaved varieties.

PURSLANE (*Portulaca oleracea*): 'Goldberger' grows well in alkaline soils (pH 7.0 to 8.0) throughout the Southwest.

SALAD BURNET (*Sanguisorba minor*): Perennial in the Upper Desert and Cool Highland Zones, it may survive in a Cold Mountain garden if mulched well for winter. Soils of Low and Middle Desert zones are too hot for this tasty green, although some grow it in those zones as a winter annual.

WATER SPINACH (*Ipomea aquatica*): Related to sweet potatoes, the scientific name lets you know this will do well with ample moisture, like in a water garden. Leaves and roots are eaten in Hong Kong.

VIOLET (*Viola odorata*): Once your violets are done blooming, don't forget about them! Violet greens are tasty in salads, and were once a popular potherb. Select delicate young leaves.

■ *When and Where to Plant*

Temperature: Warm-season greens will germinate in soil temperatures of 65°F to 85°F.

Soil: All of these greens need a rich, well-drained soil, with a pH of 6.5 to 7.5 (unless noted). Add ample compost or aged manure to the soil before planting for healthy growth. Containers also work well.

Sun: Full to afternoon shade in the Desert zones.

■ *How to Plant*

Starting seeds indoors: You can start greens seeds indoors (or on the porch) two to four weeks before you harvest the last of your cool-season greens. Be sure you acclimate your seedlings to the heat before shocking them by planting in full sun.

Planting outside: Sow seeds outdoors and cover with seed-starting mix or potting soil. Press the soil down and water. (Pressing the soil cover down helps keep the tiny seeds from floating away.) Thin to 4 inches after the plants have three sets of leaves. Thin to 12-inch spacing as the plants start to mature. Eat what you thin!

■ *How to Grow*

Water: Greens are not heavy drinkers, but keep the soil evenly moist for best flavor.

Fertilizer: Remember, "Leaves love nitrogen." All leaf crops respond well to applications of well-composted chicken or steer manure prior to planting. High nitrogen fertilizer once per month is also an option.

Pest control: The arid Southwest offers the home gardener few insect pests on these greens (yet). Quail are notorious eaters of tender young greenery. I place a screen of chicken wire over the large pots in which I grow my greens. This keeps the quail from eating young plants, and the larger leaves that grow up through the screen are too coarse for the quail.

■ *When and How to Harvest*

You can start harvesting leaves usually within three weeks after planting or when the plants have at least ten leaves on them. Cut the outermost leaves first, always leaving six leaves on the plant to produce sugars to help the plant continue growing. Use scissors or pinch off the leaves at the base of the leaf stalk. Or you can wait until plants are large and harvest the entire plant.

MELON

My childhood introduction to puns was the old joke "How do you get the water in the watermelon? You plant them in the spring." Yes, these squash family members will need ample water, but they are such a treat, especially if you are introducing small children to the joys of gardening. The ample moisture of a projected "El Niño" year is a good time to plant melons. Melons can be one of the "Three Sisters," and once introduced into our area by the Spanish were quickly adapted as such by the Native tribes. Like all the warm-season fruits, blossom-end rot is an issue, thus select smaller fruited varieties. Careful attention is also needed when selecting varieties that will produce fruit before the frost in the Upper zones and before high temperature and low humidity reduce fertility in the Desert zones. The difference in melons such as muskmelon and honeydew is flavor and skin appearance. The skin can vary from smooth to warty to "cracked." If you don't like musky flavor of muskmelon and cantaloupe, go for the sweeter melons (all the rest). Select which one on the description of flavor and days to maturity.

■ *Recommended Varieties*

CANTALOUPE/MUSKMELON (*Cucumis melo* ssp.):
  Low and Middle Desert: 'Edisto', 'Hales Best', 'Piel de Sapo', 'Planters Jumbo'.
  Upper Desert and Cool Highlands: 'Hearts of Gold', 'Ice Cream', 'Minnesota Midget', 'Pike'.
  Cold Mountains: 'Golden Jenny', 'Minnesota Midget', 'Sleeping Beauty'.

NON MUSKMELON (Casaba, Crenshaw, and Honeydew (*Cucumis melo* ssp.):
  Low and Middle Desert: 'Castillia', 'Esperanza de Oro', 'O'odham Keli Baso', 'San Juan'.
  Upper Desert and Cool Highlands: 'Corrales', 'Esperanza de Oro', 'Isleta Pueblo', 'Navajo Mix', 'Navajo Yellow', 'Ojo Caliente', 'Santo Domingo Pueblo'.
  Cold Mountains: 'Cochita', 'Corrales', 'Navajo Mix', 'Ojo Caliente', 'Santo Domingo Pueblo'.

WATERMELON (*Citrullus lanatus*):
  Low and Middle Desert: 'Crimson Sweet', 'Early Moonbeam', 'Mayo', 'Sugar Baby', 'Tohono O'odham Yellow-Meated'.
  Upper Desert and Cool Highlands: 'Hopi Yellow', 'Navajo Red-Seeded', 'Navajo Winter', 'Skiyatko', 'Tohono O'odham Yellow-Meated'.
  Cold Mountains: 'Hopi Yellow', 'Navajo Red-Seeded', 'Navajo Winter', 'Northern Star', 'Orange Glo'.

It's a good idea to place something under your cantaloupe fruit so they don't sit directly on the ground.

■ *When and Where to Plant*

Temperature: Direct-sow melon seeds in the soil when soil temperatures are at least 65°F. It's important to plant melons when the soil is warm enough, but also to allow enough time for the plants to flower before air temperatures routinely reach above 85°F during the day. This can be a short window in the Southwest.

Soil: The soil pH should be 6.2 to 7.0. The desert heirloom varieties listed above can tolerate moderately alkaline soil, up to 7.5 but melon production may suffer.

Sun: Full sun. Afternoon shade in Low Desert.

Watermelons take a lot of water, but the taste of a homegrown melon is worth it.

■ How to Plant

Plant seeds ½ inch deep in hills at least 4 feet apart, and plant three seeds per hill or better yet, water-catching basin. Thin plants to one every 3 to 4 feet after they grow three sets of leaves.

■ How to Grow

Melon plants have both male and female flowers. The flowers have to be pollinated in order to produce fruits. If you want to be absolutely sure that plants have been pollinated, you can hand-pollinate them. Move pollen from a male flower to a female flower using a paintbrush or cotton swab. (Female flowers have a small swelling behind the flower, which is what will grow into the melon.)

Water: Melons require ample water. Plan on drippers or soaker hoses, and water to a 1-foot depth every day or two. Water at dawn, and learn to identify the watersaving droop of the leaves that occurs in late afternoon. This normal droop is different from actual drought stress. If you hand water, put a tall stake next to the base of the plant. Once the vines spread all over your yard, you can still find the place to water.

Fertilizer: Start with ample compost in the soil and fertilize with a phosphorous and potassium-rich fertilizer once a month in the growing season.

Pest control: Melons suffer from the same types of pests that all squash-family plants encounter. Cucumber beetles, flea beetles, squash bugs, and squash vine borers are some of the worst. Use row covers and lift the row covers for two hours in the early morning at least twice a week to encourage pollination, or hand-pollinate. If you have bad pest problems, consider growing melons under cover for their entire growing season and hand-pollinating to ensure fruit set.

■ Harvesting

When are melons ripe? That is the hardest thing to learn and something you'll figure out over time. Save your seed packages and refer to them, as different varieties will differ in days to maturation. Since it's not easy to count back 180 days from planting, count the days from flowering. Cantaloupe is ripe generally around thirty days after flowering and they should smell sweet. Honeydews take about forty days after flowering, look for a pale green color. Watermelons may take from thirty to sixty days from flowers to fruit, depending on variety. Watch the tendril closest to the fruit. Usually when that turns brown, the watermelons are ready.

OKRA *(Abelmoschus esculentus)*

Some folks may skip this page, and that's a shame because even if you don't like the vegetable, okra has beautiful hibiscus-family flowers, and some varieties can be quite striking. I always plant a few okra to help attract pollinators to my garden (plus the dried pods make great cat toys). Yes the cooked pods do produce a mucilaginous gum, but this compound is excellent at slowing the digestion of carbohydrates and sugars, thus helping control insulin response to starchy meals. Although that may not sound very appetizing (mucilage?!), okra is quite delicious if prepared correctly.

Okra is a key ingredient in gumbo and tastes wonderful when brushed with olive oil and tossed on the grill (keep the summer kitchen cool). Do you make your own pickles? Even folks who say they don't like okra seem to be willing to choke down some pickled okra just fine. Although considered a "Southern" vegetable, this relative of cotton does well in the warm Southwestern garden in the long growing season of the Desert zones.

■ Recommended Varieties

'Beck's Gardenville', 'Eagle Pass', 'Guarijio', and 'Texas Hill Country Red' all do well in the lower humidity of the Southwest.

■ When and Where to Plant

Temperature: Warm soils, meaning 80°F to 95°F. Okra will be difficult to grow to maturity in the Cool Highlands. In the Cold Mountains, use your space for a different crop.

Soil: Soil pH of 6.0 to 8.0 is fine for okra. It can be grown in poor, even somewhat clay soils. Rotate the planting location of okra from year to year to keep plants from suffering from soilborne diseases.

Sun: Full sun. Plants get tall, so plant on the north side of the garden so that they won't shade other plants reaching for the sun.

■ How to Plant

Starting seeds indoors: Not ideal, but four to six weeks before last frost if you must, in a plantable pot if possible.

Planting outside: If planting transplants, try not to disturb the roots—okra is finicky. Use scissors to cut the pot away from the plant, rather than yanking the plant out of the pot. Sow seed ¾ inch deep, 4 inches apart. Thin or space transplants 9 to 12 inches apart. It is helpful to soak the seeds overnight before planting outside to ensure good germination.

■ *How to Grow*

Water: Water to a depth of 8 to 12 inches and then allow soil to dry somewhat between watering.

Fertilizer: Fertilize once during the growing season with a balanced fertilizer.

Pest control: One more reason to grow okra—no major pest problems.

■ *When and How to Harvest*

Harvest okra when the pods are young and tender, usually 2 to 3 inches long. The larger the pod, the tougher it will be, and the less palatable. Once an okra plant starts producing pods large enough to harvest, it can keep going until frost or it wears itself out. Plan to pick new pods every single day to keep production going. If you miss the daily harvest, and pods get too large, pick them off and dry them for cat toys or craft projects (painted right, they look like a Santa—complete with hat). Or you can compost large pods, but leaving them on the plant will signal the plant to stop producing.

Okra fresh from the garden is best for roasting or frying.

A stake or tomato cage for your pepper plants will help support the plants as the peppers ripen and grow heavy.

PEPPERS, SWEET & HOT
(Capsicum annuum)

Like eggplants and tomatoes, peppers are members of the deadly nightshade family. The only part of the plant that is edible is the fruit. Never eat the flowers or the leaves—they're poisonous. (Not that you would, but if there's one plant that you don't want to experiment with, it's nightshades.) There are hundreds of varieties to grow—from bell peppers to banana peppers, from hot to sweet, mild to burning. As with most of these warm-season vegetables, almost every variety of pepper will grow equally well in the Southwest. It's expensive to buy fresh peppers at the grocery, so learning how to grow these vegetables can have a significant impact on your shopping bill.

■ *Recommended Varieties*

With peppers, both sweet and hot, the smaller-fruited varieties will resist blossom-end rot better than giant fruits.

Bell peppers come in many colors—green, red, black, chocolate, orange, yellow. Select a variety that matures within the number of growing days. This is especially critical in the Cool Highlands and Cold Mountains. That said, here are some of my favorites that should be able to be grown throughout our area: 'Sweet Cherry' (red), 'California Wonder' (green to red), 'Kevin's Early Orange', 'Purple Beauty', 'Sweet Banana' (progresses from green, to yellow, to red).

Chili (hot) peppers come in many grades of heat, measured in "Scovilles." The higher the number, the hotter. Try the mother from which all were bred, the chiltepin. I wear disposable nitrile gloves when harvesting these, and everyone should take care not to touch eyes or any skin on your body. For less heat (in descending order): 'Chili Piquin', 'Scotch Bonnet', 'Jalapeno', 'Habanero', 'Green Chili'.

Also consider these pepper varieties used for flavor but not hot: 'Pimento Select', 'Early Hungarian Sweet', and 'Hungarian Paprika.'

■ *When and Where to Plant*

Temperature: Peppers need warm soil to grow—at least 65°F to 75°F.

Soil: Soil pH depends on variety and can be from 5.5 to 7.8. The sweet peppers do better at the acid end of the range, while the Southwestern Heirloom hot chilies do better on the alkaline end of the range.

Sun: Full sun in the upper elevations, afternoon shade in the Desert zones.

Some bell peppers can be left on the plant longer for a red or orange color.

■ *Where and How to Plant*

Starting seeds indoors: Due to the summer heat and low humidity making the flowers infertile, it's advantageous to start seeds indoors or purchase transplants so your plants will produce before the real heat of summer. Start seeds indoors six weeks before you plan to transplant your 6-inch seedlings outside (four weeks before last frost).

Planting outside: Plant pepper seed ¼ inch deep. It helps to cover them with a dark-colored seed-starter soil to help warm them and get them growing. I space seeds about 2 inches apart and thin later, selecting the most vigorous growers. Plant transplants 12 inches apart.

■ *How to Grow*

Our low humidity will make producing peppers a challenge. I place a tomato cage over my peppers and cover it with shade cloth held in

Banana peppers are easy to grow!

Stake plants or cage individually when they grow to heights of 18 inches or taller.

place with clothespins. In early morning, I moisten the plants and the cloth by spritzing with a jet of water from the hose. This raises the relative humidity and slightly cools the area, improving pollen viability and stigma receptivity. Be sure not to cover the plant entirely or the pollinators can't visit.

Water: Regular water required! If peppers (sweet or hot) go through wet/dry/wet/dry cycles, they develop blossom-end rot.

Fertilizer: All kinds of peppers produce best with a balanced fertilizer every three to four weeks through the growing season.

Pest control: Peppers are relatively pest free, except for our Southwestern birds. (There are a number of wild red fruits they are too used to eating.) As mentioned, I place a tomato cage around the plants when they are small, this makes it easy to add bird netting (clipped on with clothespins) once pepper fruits near maturity.

When and How to Harvest

Refer to your seed packet or plant tag—it will state days to maturity, as well as pictures of what the finished product looks like. Some red bell peppers are green when they're immature and turn red eventually. Some bell peppers never turn red. Hungarian wax peppers can be picked when green or red. It gets confusing. The longer peppers grow, the more they develop their flavor, be it sweet or hot.

SQUASH, SUMMER *(Cucurbita pepo)*

"Back East" they joke about having too much zucchini and other summer squashes, but seriously, it is hard to have that problem in the arid Southwest where our high summer temperatures impact the pollen fertility and reduce or eliminate fruit production. But if you do luck out with some cooperative summer weather, you will end up with an ample harvest. Not to worry— these soft-skinned summer squash freeze easily. Shredded or cubed and sealed in quart bags, your squash will be ready for use in chocolate zucchini bread, winter stews, ratatouille, squash pie, etc. (No need to blanch or steam if slices are thin.) I always run out of squash long before the end of winter.

■ *Recommended Varieties*

I like to plant varieties that are yellow when ripe, since they are easier to find amongst the green leaves.

When possible, purchase varieties that are resistant to cucumber mosaic virus (CMV). The mildews, powdery mildew (PM) and downy mildew (DM), are less of an issue unless we have massive monsoons.

'Chayote' can only be grown in Low Desert. 'Early White Bush Scallop Patty Pan' can be grown only in Cool Highlands and Cold Mountains. The rest of these miscellaneous soft-skinned squash can be grown throughout the Southwest: 'Black Beauty Zucchini', 'Costata Romanesca Zucchini', 'Dark Star Zucchini', 'Early Golden Crookneck', 'Early Prolific Straightneck', 'Golden Bush Scallop Patty Pan', 'Green Tint Patty Pan', 'Grey Zucchini', and 'Tromboncino Heirloom.'

You can harvest summer squash right after the flower on the end of the fruit wilts.

■ When and Where to Plant

Temperature: Plant outside when soil temperatures are at least 65°F.

Soil: These non-native squash grow best in well-drained soil with a pH of 5.5 to 6.5. With our soils you will need to add ample compost to the soil before planting.

Sun: Full sun to afternoon shade in Low and Middle Desert.

■ How to Plant

Starting seeds indoors: Squash plants are difficult to transplant. If you want to get a jump on the season, start seeds indoors two weeks before you want to plant outdoors. Plant the seeds in peat pots or biodegradable pots that you can plant directly in the ground without removing the plants.

Planting outside: Planting depth depends on variety, plant twice as deep as seeds are long, thus ½ to 1 inch deep. You can plant two to three seeds per hole. When seedlings are 3 inches tall, use scissors to thin to two plants per 12 inches. As plants grow, you can further reduce this to one plant per 18 or 24 inches. This overplanting gives you more plants to work with if you have problems with pests.

■ How to Grow

Water: Keep squashes evenly moist. It helps if you mulch the garden after the plants germinate.

Fertilizer: Sidedress with a balanced fertilizer every three weeks during the growing season.

Pest control: Avoid squash vine borer infestation by smearing the base of the stem with petroleum jelly or wrapping it in aluminum foil. Cucumber beetles and squash beetles can be controlled with row covers when plants are young. You can raise the covers for two hours in the early morning to allow in the bees needed for pollination, or hand pollinate your plants.

■ When and How to Harvest

Once summer squash plants start producing, you need to check the plants daily for fruits to harvest. Summer squash tastes better when harvested young. You can even harvest with the flowers still hanging on to the ends of the fruits. Use your scissors, pruners or a knife to cut the fruit, leaving around ½ inch of stem. Like all other warm-season crops, if you leave the fruits on the plant too long, they develop mature seeds and can become bitter tasting. Pick off these too-large fruit to encourage plants to produce new fruit.

SQUASH, WINTER *(Cucurbita* spp.*)*

Winter squash is a broad term referring to the squash family members that have hard skins and thus keep longer in "winter" storage. Depending on when you planted them, these squash may be ready to harvest it the middle of summer—between July and September. Harvest them! Although they have hard skins, don't leave them in the garden past their maturity date or they can become sun-baked and inedible. Winter squash includes some species that began cultivation here in the New World, plus Old World favorites. Plant breeders have been hard at work, so there are many to select from, including such favorites as acorn, butternut, delicata, and others. These plants grow in much the same way as summer squash, but the fruits take longer to mature. Gourds are included here as they have the same growth needs.

All winter squash will cross readily with other squash family members, making seed saving not an option without a great deal of labor. Luckily, all winter squash and pumpkins (but not all the gourds) have edible and tasty seeds rich in protein, vitamins, and minerals. Toast your squash seeds (called pepitas) and enjoy them as a snack instead of popcorn.

■ *Recommended Varieties*

Like other summer fruits, smaller-fruited varieties are best in the Southwest to avoid issues with blossom-end rot. The varieties listed here tend to have smaller leaves, and thus they are less likely to sun scald, plus will use less water. If in doubt, check the days to maturity and select accordingly.

Low Desert: 'Carrizo', 'Gila Pima Hal', 'Guarijio Segualca', 'Mayo Blusher', 'Tahiti Melon'.

Middle Desert: 'Carrizo', 'Calabaza Mexicana', 'Guarijio Segualca', 'Kikuza', 'Papalote Ranch Cushaw', 'Tarahumara', 'Tohono O'odham Hal'.

High Desert: 'Calabaza Mexicana', 'Magdalena Big Cheese', 'Papalote Ranch Cushaw', 'Waltham Butternut'.

Cool Highlands 'Acoma Pumpkin', 'Hopi Pumpkin', 'Navajo Gray Hubbard', 'Waltham Butternut'.

Cold Mountains: 'Acoma Pumpkin', 'Hopi Pumpkin', 'Penasco Cheese' (from Penasco, New Mexico), 'Waltham Butternut'.

GOURDS

Gourds are fun to grow, dry, and then decorate or cut open for birdhouses, planters, drums, and more. The smaller ones can be creatively transformed by children into all manner of "critters" with paint and imagination. (Grandma will treasure such homemade holiday ornaments!) These varieties will do well in the Southwest: 'Hopi Rattle', 'Mayo Warty Blue', 'O'odham Dipper', 'Peyote Rattle', and 'Tepehuan Canteen.'

When and Where to Plant

Temperature: Plant outside when soil temperatures are at least 65°F.

Soil: The pH range is 5.5 to 7.5, depending on variety. Varieties developed by the Native farmers tolerate our more alkaline soils well. Otherwise, add ample compost to the soil before planting, and consider a raised bed.

Sun: Full sun, to afternoon shade in Low and Middle Desert gardens.

Winter squash can be grown as an edible or as a decorative gourd.

How to Plant

Starting seeds indoors: Winter squash plants dislike transplanting. Start seeds indoors two to four weeks before you want to plant outdoors and use pots you can place directly in the ground without removing the plants.

Planting outside: Plant two to three seeds per hole, ½ to 1 inch deep (the bigger the seed, the deeper). When seedlings are 3 inches tall, use scissors to thin to two plants per 12 inches. As plants grow, you can further reduce to one plant per 24 or 48 inches. (Overplanting slightly gives you more plants to work with if you have problems with pests.)

How to Grow

Water: Keep squashes moist and mulch the garden after the plants germinate.

Fertilizer: Apply a balanced fertilizer every three weeks in the growing season.

Pest control: Like all the squash family, squash vine borers, squash bugs, cucumber beetles, and Mexican bean beetles plague squash plants. Plant borer-resistant small-vined varieties as recommended here. Wrap the base of the vine with foil or smear with petroleum jelly. Use row covers when plants are young to protect plants from flying pests. You can raise the covers for two hours in the early morning a few days a week to allow insects to reach the flowers for pollination.

When and How to Harvest

Harvest winter squashes when their skin has thickened (hard to tell) and become dull and no longer shiny. Cut them from the vine, leaving 1 inch of their stem. (This helps prevent fruit desiccation.) Wipe off any soil. Use a clean cloth dipped in a dilute bleach solution to wipe down the skin to kill any bacteria or fungus. Store in a cool, dark place below 65°F (or under the bed) and then don't forget to use them! You can store for three to six months or just until one week before they become wrinkly.

SWEET POTATO *(Ipomoea batatas)*

Sweet potatoes are fun to grow, but not everyone can grow them because they are warm-season plants that are highly sensitive to cold weather and require a long, frost-free growing season. But they taste so good! If you have a minimum of 90—ideally 120—frost-free days, you should dedicate a corner of your garden to growing some sweet potatoes. This means you can grow them in the Low and Middle Desert, and into the High Desert. If you have a sunny warm south-facing corner, you may be able to get sweet potatoes in Cool Highland gardens. Sorry, there are not enough reliably frost-free days in the Cold Mountains to grow this crop.

For those with enough frost-free days, plant sweet potatoes in spring, provide water, enjoy the luscious foliage, and come autumn, dig up a bountiful harvest to last through the winter. Technically sweet potatoes are tubers, stem tissue that is swollen and stores nutrients. Grown from sprouts or cuttings termed slips (or draws) this is a fun one for kids to grow. Avoid planting supermarket sweet potatoes, since you do not know how long they take to fully mature and develop their sweetness, plus they may carry soil pathogens into your garden.

■ *Recommended Varieties*

High Desert: Choose from these more quickly maturing varieties: 'Beauregard', 'Georgia Jet', or 'O'Henry.' Middle and Low Desert can select any of the above plus 'All Purple', 'Bunch Porto Rico' (good in small gardens), and 'Ginseng.'

■ *When and Where to Plant*

Temperature: Plant outside two weeks after last frost date, and when the soil temperature is at least 65°F.

Soil: Sweet potatoes need well-drained soil that is acidic with a pH of 5.5 to 6.5. If you have clay soil, amend heavily with compost and sand or plant in raised beds. They can also be grown in deep containers on the patio.

Sun: Full sun to afternoon shade in Low and Middle Desert. Consider planting these in the landscape under trees that provide filtered shade, like palo verdes.

■ *How to Plant*

Starting indoors: Sweet potatoes are grown from sprouts, called slips. Slips are created by suspending a "seed" sweet potato in a jar of water. A number of stems with roots will emerge, and you will "slip" these off the seed potato and plant them. (You can also buy slips.) Once you have grown sweet potatoes in your garden, keep a few of the better growing ones and grow your own slips in following years.

Planting outside: Plant slips when the soil temperature is at least 65°F. Plant slips 4 inches deep and 14 to 18 inches apart in rows 36 inches apart.

How to Grow

Water: Water will be needed for these plants with large leaf area. But not too much, they do like to dry somewhat between watering.

Fertilizer: Like many root crops, sweet potatoes do not need a lot of fertilizer. Ample compost will provide the nutrients they need through the growing season.

Pest control: Sweet potatoes are largely pest free, especially if you plant resistant varieties. If you plan to grow sweet potatoes each year, keep problems at bay by rotating where you plant them.

When and How to Harvest

Sweet potatoes are ready to harvest 90 to 120 days after planting or when the tuber is close to 3 inches in diameter. Gently dig around the tubers and free them from the soil. Cut off the vines leaving a ¼-inch stem. (You can then compost the vines.) In the southeast they dry the tubers for a day or two on top of the soil, but this is not advisable in our climate. Bring the tubers inside to "cure" for a week before putting them in long-term storage. To cure, set the potatoes, not touching, in a warm dark area, like a garage. Curing allows bruises and cuts to heal. For storage move them to a cool (55°F to 65°F), dark area, and leave them alone until you're ready to use them.

Sweet potatoes grow best in a long growing season and warm weather.

TOMATILLO *(Physalis philadelphica)*

Also called "husk tomato," tomatillos are totally yummy tomato relatives that develop their fruit inside a papery shell. A very close and also edible kin is the ground cherry (*Physalis pruinosa*). Both are members of the deadly nightshade family, and there are a number of nonedible relatives of these garden treats, including the beautiful but deadly "Chinese lantern flower" (*Physalis alkekengi*). Luckily, tomatillo and ground cherries are not only edible but also extremely palatable. You can savor them fresh off the bush, roasted, sauted, or made into salsa. (My husband loves mild tomatillo salsa on his morning scrambled eggs, and I can't grow enough for him.)

Depending on variety, tomatillos can be tart or sweet, large or small, and tasty either raw or cooked. If you cook the large green varieties, it helps develop their complex flavor and sweetness. Once cooked they can be preserved with canning. Tomatillos are ridiculously easy to grow from seed, and the small, sweet-fruited varieties, including the ground cherry, are a great starter plant for kids. One final plus, these are good in containers. Each plant is prolific, so a few seeds go a long way! There are a number of wild species of tomatillo that grow throughout the Southwest and plants are readily cross-fertile. This is to warn you that seed saving is not an option in the Southwest, without bagging flowers and hand pollination.

Note: The former scientific name for tomatillo was *Physalis ixocarpa*, and it is still sometimes sold by that name.

■ Recommended Varieties

GROUND CHERRY: 'Cossack Pineapple' and 'Goldie' work well.

TOMATILLOS:

Low Desert and Middle Desert: 'De Milpa', 'Purple', 'Tomate Verde'.

High Desert and upper elevations: 'Dr. Wyche's Yellow', 'Monntain Pima', 'Tepehuan', 'Zuni'.

Cool Highlands and Cold Mountains: Can consider the so-called "Cape Gooseberry" *Physalis peruviana*, originally from Peru, imported to the Cape of South Africa and reintroduced to us.

■ When and Where to Plant

Temperature: Soil temperature of 70°F to 80°F.

Soil: The soil pH should be 6.0 to 7.0. Garden tomatillos grow best in well-drained soil. If you have clay soil, amend with sand and ample compost before planting.

Sun: Full sun to afternoon shade in the Desert zones.

■ How to Plant

Starting seeds indoors: You only need to plant tomatillo seeds indoors if you grow them in the Cold Mountain zone. Start seeds inside four to six weeks before you plan to plant outside.

Planting outside: Plant seeds ¼ inch deep, once the soil temperature is at least 60°F. Cover lightly with seed-starting mix, and keep moist. When the plants are 3 inches tall, thin to allow 12 inches between plants.

■ How to Grow

Water: Keep tomatillos evenly moist. Wet/dry/wet/dry cycles can cause blossom-end rot in the larger varieties.

Fertilizer: Not necessary. Optionally use a balanced fertilizer four weeks after planting. You can also add a bloom or fruiting fertilizer once they begin to flower.

Pest control: Keep an eye out for pests that attack tomatoes, such as tomato hornworms. Cutworms are also an issue. You can protect plants from cutworms by wrapping the bottom 3 inches of the stems with foil or newspaper.

■ When and How to Harvest

Tomatillos are generally ripe when the husks start to turn tan and dry out, but this is not the case with all varieties. Look for fruits that fill their husk. A gentle tug should release any ripe fruit into your hand. Enjoy fresh or hunt the internet for some wonderful canning recipes. Tomatillos can be husked and placed whole in freezer bags for later use. Toss a few frozen tomatillos in the pan first when you make stir fry with your winter greens—yum!

TOMATO *(Lycopersicon esculentum)*

Nothing beats the taste of a fresh-picked tomato from the garden, but this member of the nightshade family is extremely hard to grow in the Southwest. Low humidity and high temperatures often lead to failure to set fruit, and even nonviable pollen. Above 95°F and the plants will not even flower. Tomato plants need a great deal of expensive water to grow, there are a number of pests that attack them, and blossom-end rot is a persistent problem. I don't often waste the space and water on them, but since Americans are tomato crazy, here are some tips that might lead to success in your garden.

■ *Recommended Varieties*

Small and cherry tomatoes are recommended for the Southwest, due to blossom-end rot. The summer weather with hot, dry winds and periodic humid flushes in monsoon season is all just too much for most varieties of tomato. You also need to select varieties resistant to the common diseases that plague tomatoes, like verticillium wilt, fusarium wilt, and root knot nematodes, tobacco mosaic virus, and many more.

With all those cautions, these varieties have been shown to do well in the Southwest: 'Ciudad Victoria', 'Flamenco', 'Green Grape', 'Nichols Heirloom', 'Prescott Heirloom', 'Punta Banda', 'Texas Wild Cherry', and 'Yellow Pear'. Smallest of all, and closest genetically to wild tomatoes are the currant tomatoes like 'Red Currant' and 'Sugar Cherry', and these are quite successful.

■ *When and Where to Plant*

Temperature: Soil temperature of 70°F to 80°F.

Soil: The soil pH should be 6.0 to 7.0. Add ample compost and a slow-release, organic fertilizer before planting.

Sun: Full sun to afternoon shade in Desert gardens.

■ *How to Plant*

Starting seeds indoors: Start seeds indoors six weeks before you want to plant tomatoes outdoors. Harden off plants before planting them in the garden. Plant transplants 5 inches deep to encourage rooting from the stem and thus developing a deep root system.

Planting outside: You can direct-sow tomatoes in Desert regions. Sow seeds and cover with ¼ inch of seed-starting mix. Keep the seeds moist while sprouting—you may have to water twice a day. As the plants start growing, thin to 18 to 24 inches apart. Place cages and supports once the plants are 6 inches tall. Hill up the soil around the bottom 6 inches of each plant stem to encourage strong roots.

◼ *How to Grow*

Our low humidity will make producing tomatoes a challenge. I place a tomato cage over my plants when they are tiny and cover it with shade cloth held in place with clothespins. In early morning, I moisten the plants and the cloth by spritzing with a jet of water from the hose. This raises the relative humidity and slightly cools the area, improving pollen viability and stigma receptivity. Be sure to not entirely cover the plant or the pollinators can't visit.

Water: Tomatoes need steady, consistent moisture in order to avoid blossom-end rot, a cultural problem (caused by the plant care, not by a fungus). Use soaker hoses or drippers to make it easier to water tomatoes deeply, and mulch well with pine needles, palo verde leaves or clean straw. Water to 18 inches deep, and you should only need to water every other day.

Fertilizer: Avoid high-nitrogen fertilizer, which can cause more leaf growth than flower development. Use a bloom or fruit fertilizer once plants start flowering.

Pest control: Almost every pest alive enjoys eating tomatoes. Growing resistant varieties helps prevent many pest problems. Keep an eye out for tomato hornworms—big green caterpillars as large as your thumb. Pick them off and squash them, or like I do, drop them into a bucket of soapy water. Do not feed these caterpillars to your koi! Hornworms have become toxic by eating the foliage of this deadly nightshade. Even roadrunners know better than to eat them.

For best results, keep tomatoes consistently and evenly watered.

Toward the end of the season, cover plants with bird netting so these avian pests do not peck holes in every single one of the ripening fruits.

◼ *When and How to Harvest*

Tomatoes are ripe when you need little effort to pull them off the plant. Leave tomatoes on the plant for as long as possible for the sweetest fruits.

Warm-Season Herbs

Technically, all of the herbs in this section are perennial plants that live for many years. The problem is that they mostly come from somewhere else in the world, and a few are not entirely adapted to life in the Southwest. Nonetheless, a number of the herbs in this section are commonly used in landscaping, and you may encounter them in traffic medians or in front of your doctor's office. Think of the abuse they suffer in such harsh areas, and realize that growing these tough plants can be a good way to ease into gardening. (You should not harvest herbs grown in such public spaces—who knows how they are contaminated?)

Perennial plants including trees, shrubs, and herbs are best planted in our area in early autumn, when they will have enough time to get well-established before the heat of next summer. The next best time to plant perennials is in early spring. If in doubt, plant any of these warm-season herbs in spring after the last frost date for your area. Two of the herbs in this section, basil and epazote, are from the tropics and rarely survive any Southwestern winter, no matter how mild. On the other end of the spectrum is mint. Originally from northern climates, mint is genetically programmed to go dormant in winter, no matter how relatively warm it may be.

Dry Your Own Herbs

Drying your own herbs is easy and highly satisfying. There are just a few simple steps.

Herbs are usually best picked when they are unstressed, which is in the morning, not at the end of a long hot, tiring day. Select clean, healthy, pest-free plant material.

Rinse the herbs well with either a hose, or after you cut them off the plant, under the tap. Shake well or gently pat with a towel to remove excess water.

Dry herbs out of direct sunlight, and in such a manner to allow air movement. There are four ways you can do this: flat on a screen, tied into small bundles and hung from the ceiling, placed into a large terracotta clay saucer, or in a dehydrator, as long as the temperature remains low enough.

Mint and thyme both grow well in the Southwest.

ALOYSIA *(Aloysia* spp.*)*

You have eaten this herb if you have dined in Mexican restaurants. Aloysia species are one of a random number of species known as "Mexican oregano." Why I advocate growing this over any other oregano is because it is a lovely, low-water landscape shrub that is wonderfully fragrant, long-blooming, and will attract butterflies as well as bees to the garden. Arching vase-shaped shrubs that grow 3 to 5 feet high and as wide, several species are found in the wild across the Southwest. Since they are native plants hardly any "gardening" is actually required. Plant them in the landscape and enjoy them, harvesting as needed for use and to keep them trimmed to size. I grab a handful of twigs and leaves to give the barbecue grill a good scrub before cooking. This helps clean the grill and leaves some tasty oils to flavor what we grill (tastes great with grilled eggplant). Aloysias are in the Verbena family, and like most members of the family are rich in nectar and are very attractive to many pollinators, including butterflies and the docile solitary desert bees.

Recommended Varieties

For Cool Highlands and lower elevations, look in the nurseries for plants sold with the scientific names of *Aloysia gratissima, A. lycioides,* or *A. wrightii. Aloysia schultzii*, from southern Sonora will only survive the relative cold of the Low and possibly Middle Desert. *Aloysia* will not survive in Cold Mountain gardens.

When and Where to Plant

Plants are available in 1-gallon pots at local nurseries.

Temperature: Aloysia are subtropical shrubs, and as subtropicals, they are cold deciduous, often losing their leaves below 20°F. Do not be alarmed, and avoid watering them in the cooler months. Since they lose their leaves in winter, they are better for a background plant in most landscapes.

Soil: Aloysias do best in well-drained soil, pH 6.5 to 7.5.

Sun: Full sun in upper elevations, part or filtered shade, especially on summer afternoons in the Low and Middle Desert.

How to Grow

Water: Aloysia are watered at least once a day in nursery pots—you will need to taper this off as they become established in the garden. Once established, water to 2 feet deep twice a month in summer, more often in sandier soil. Have care, aloysia prefer to dry out somewhat between waterings. If the roots stay too wet, they can rot.

Fertilizer: This desert native does not require fertilizer, but if you enjoy the floral fragrance or are a beekeeper, a flowering fertilizer can be applied at half-strength through the summer months to encourage more prolific flowering.

Harvesting and Use

Harvest leaves for drying anytime. Leaves can also be used fresh but may taste mildly bitter. Like bay leaves, drying appears to eliminate some of the bitter flavor. Store in a sealed container out of direct sunlight and use within eighteen months.

Aloysia flowers are fragrant and attract helpful pollinators to the garden.

BASIL *(Ocimum spp., primarily Ocimum basilicum)*

Basil has a long and very rich tradition of use. The word comes from the Greek, meaning "king," and indeed, basil is considered the "king of herbs" by many chefs. Basil is originally native to Iran, India and other tropical regions of Asia, having been cultivated there for more than 5,000 years. The species used in Italian food is typically called sweet basil (*Ocimum basilicum*), as opposed to Asian basils, including Thai basil (*O. basilicum* var. *thyrsiflora*), lemon basil (*O. × citriodorum*) and holy basil (*O. sanctum*). Basil is a useful crop for garden wildlife. Rabbits avoid the plants, making it a good barrier crop. Native solitary bees visit the nectar-rich flowers. Seed-eating birds, especially the charming and colorful lesser goldfinch, adore the oil rich seeds.

Last, basil is not an easy plant for all people to grow. It's a good thing that there are over 150 varieties to select from. You may need to try several varieties until you find the one that does well for you in your yard and style of plant care. For my tendency toward Darwinistic gardening, and the clay soils in my yard, the 'Queen of Siam' basil works for me.

■ *Recommended Varieties*

Varieties with smaller leaves are recommended for our low humidity, otherwise plants can be overly stressed and suffer pest problems. For our alkaline soils, you can't beat 'Mrs. Burns' Famous Lemon Basil'. Also consider 'Greek Yevani', 'Lime', 'Mayo', 'Napoletano', 'Purple Petra', 'Siam Queen', and 'Yoeme'. For Cold Mountains, try 'African Blue' which is a fairly cold-tolerant basil that you can grow on a sunny windowsill during winter.

■ *When and Where to Plant*

Temperature: Plant outside when nighttime temperatures are consistently 70°F or above.

Soil: Soil for basil should be a rich, well-drained loamy soil that is high in organic matter. Sandy soils drain too quickly and clay soils become waterlogged and don't hold oxygen well. Either case makes for unhappy basil plants. Ideal soil pH is 6.2 to 7.0. Add ample organic matter or grow basil in large containers with potting soil.

Sun: Basil plants prefer eight hours per day of light, but it's best to provide noon or afternoon shade in the Low and Middle Desert gardens.

■ *How to Plant*

Starting seeds indoors: Start seeds indoors two to six weeks before planting outdoors.

Planting outside: Plant transplants 12 to 18 inches apart, depending on the mature size of the variety.

■ *How to Grow*

Water: Water needs keep basil off the xeriscape plant list. Provide ample moisture for healthy flavorful, not bitter, basil. Basil that tastes bitter is a sign of water stress.

Fertilizer: Basil does best with high levels of nitrogen mixed with all the other major and minor nutrients. Our desert soils lack only the nitrogen. Adding ample organic matter or growing basil in containers generally solves this, but additional fertilizer yields large lush plants.

■ *Harvesting and Use.*

Basil is commonly used fresh in cooked recipes. It is generally added at the last moment, as cooking quickly destroys the flavor. The fresh herb can be kept for a short time in plastic bags in the refrigerator. Freezing leaves or prepared pesto is an option; both are best used within a few months. Dried basil loses much of its flavor, but is still useful as an herb. Pesto can be processed as a canned condiment and in my experience is still flavorful a year later.

BAY *(Laurus nobilis)*

In ancient Greece and Rome, the bay tree was considered sacred to Apollo, the sun deity. Leafy branches of bay were woven into wreaths to crown the heads of kings and queens, priests, priestesses, poets, bards, and the victors of battles and athletic or scholarly contests. At the first Olympics in 776 B.C.E., laurel garlands were presented to the champions of each contest.

During the Renaissance, doctors, upon passing their final examinations, were decorated with berried branches of bay. From this ancient custom derives the French word *baccalaureate* (from "bacca," a berry, and "laureus," of laurel); this has been modified into the term "bachelor" in referring to one type of college degree.

The bay laurel is an evergreen tree with glossy, deep green leaves. It grows well in arid climates such as Greece, Italy, southern France, and here in the Southwest. Bay is a lovely tree for the yard or even poolside. Growing slowly to form a stately tree, in the very best conditions it will eventually reach 40 feet high (it takes decades). The only problem with bay is that young trees are frost tender, and must be protected much like a citrus tree. You can grow bay in a container when it is young and move it onto a protected porch for the winter. Plant it out once the plant has some size as it is less likely to freeze, or you can keep it in a container for years. Indeed, you can also grow bay indoors, if you have a well-lit space.

■ *Recommended Varieties*

Be sure you buy true bay laurel. Landscape plants sold as "laurel" may be *Prunus laurocerasus*, also called the English or cherry laurel; a member of the rose family.

■ *When and Where to Plant*

Temperature: Plants may be kept outdoors in any nonfreezing month.
Soil: Bay laurels prefer well-drained soil and tolerate a pH from 6.2 to 7.5.
Sun: Full sun to part shade in summer in lower elevations.

■ *How to Plant*

Starting seeds indoors: If you can find seed of bay laurel, please let me know!
Planting outside: Purchase nursery stock (rooted cuttings) and plant outdoors in any nonfreezing month. You can also plant as a container plant and move it outdoors in summer and indoors during freezing months, indeed, this is how you will have to grow it in the Cold Mountains and Cool Highlands. In Low and Middle Desert, plant

bay outside in the landscape. In the Upper Desert, plant bay in a sheltered location that will not get much below 18°F in the winter. Since courtyards are a Southwestern tradition, if you have one, grace it with a bay tree.

How to Grow

Water: Once established, bay laurel does best if the soil is allowed to dry somewhat between watering.

Fertilizer: Bay grows well with a well-balanced fertilizer three times a year, Memorial Day, Fourth of July, and Labor Day. In Upper Desert, skip the last one as it would encourage new growth too close to frost.

Pest control: Bay is not susceptible to pests.

Harvesting and Use

Bay as a flavoring herb is always used dried. Some books say to use bay leaves fresh, but please—not true bay laurel. The Delphi Oracles chewed fresh bay leaves for visions, and a number of them died in the process. Also, there are several bitter-tasting compounds which are lost with drying, leaving the flavorful and useful oils. Leaves are used whole and removed prior to serving as they leave a bitter taste if chewed. Add bay to your cooking, or prepare as an infusion base for soups. Bay leaves are also used as a pest repellent for flour weevils. Just add several leaves, ideally in a muslin bag, to your flour canisters. Change to fresh leaves every six months. Use the old leaves as organic mulch in the garden. Bay leaves, either fresh or dried, can be used to create lovely, long-lasting herbal wreaths.

Bay laurel is a small tree or large shrub.

193

EPAZOTE *(Chenopodium ambrosioides)*

Epazote will reseed readily throughout the garden.

By the time of contact between the New and Old Worlds, epazote had been cultivated for well over a thousand years in southern and southeast coastal Mexico. It was, and still is, a principal flavoring for a large number of Yucatan and Veracruz dishes, and is indispensable for cooking black beans. Epazote, like the Old World herbs cumin and ginger, has the unique ability to help break down hard-to-digest vegetable proteins. These difficult proteins are found most often in beans, peas, and members of the cabbage family. A few leaves of epazote cooked in the pot with the potential offender can go a long way toward rendering the bean proteins, well, shall we say, "ungaseous." Epazote was brought into our area with Father Kino and is recorded as planted in the gardens at San Xavier del Bac Mission. Epazote found its way into eastern North America and Canada under the name American wormseed, Jesuit tea, Mexican tea, and Jerusalem oak. Epazote can reach 5 feet tall, but will be scraggly and unattractive. Pinch epazote plants often, especially the central branches, to keep it around 2 to 3 feet tall, compact, leafy, and with an appealing form in the garden. Epazote reseeds readily, so remove the seed stalks, or be ready to ruthlessly weed out excess plants next spring. On the other hand, seed heads turn an attractive bronze in autumn, and the lesser goldfinches enjoy the seeds. Ideally, find a less used corner of the garden for epazote, where if seeds spread they will not be a major problem. A strongly scented herb, epazote is reported as a deer repellent, and I can report that javalina, jackrabbits, cottontails, and ground squirrels avoid eating the plants.

Recommended Varieties

There are currently no varieties offered. You may see it sold as *Dysphania ambrosioides*, a former scientific name.

When and Where to Plant

Temperature: Plant epazote from seed in spring once night temperatures rise above the low 50s°F. You can also start indoors and transplant once danger of frost is past.

Soil: Soil can be poor, even clay, but plants grow best in average, well-drained soils with pH 6.2 to 7.5. Epazote can be grown in containers that are at least a foot deep.

Sun: Epazote plants do well in full sun, but some afternoon shade is appreciated in our area by this tropical herb.

How to Plant

Starting seeds indoors: Up to six weeks prior to planting outside, but in Desert gardens, simply plant outside. Seeds can take as long as four weeks to germinate.

Planting outside: Sow the tiny seeds ¼ inch deep and cover with seed-starting mix. Keep evenly moist and thin to 8 to 12 inches apart once true leaves begin to show.

How to Grow

Plants will thrive through the warm season and freeze to the ground at 35°F, but often regrow from the roots. At 20°F the roots will be killed as well.

Water: Some water is needed for this nondesert plant, especially if you want lush growth.

Fertilizer: None required.

Pests: No pests, indeed an extract of epazote is the active ingredient of the pesticide Requiem.

Harvesting and Use

Epazote is best used fresh for culinary purposes. Chop or mince leaves and add early to dishes that require long cooking, like beans, roasts, soups, or stews. Use 1 tablespoon minced leaves per cup of beans or to a 2-pound roast. Do not use as a garnish, the taste is bitter. If not fresh, frozen epazote may be used as a culinary herb, but epazote does not have the same "digestive" effect after drying.

Grow mint in a pot to prevent it from taking over the garden.

MINT *(Mentha spp.)*

Mints are a wonderful herb for many uses: tea, jelly, salads, candy-making, medicine, and more. They are many mints to choose from, in fact well over 100 species and varieties are found around the world. Add to this number the cultivars and hybrids that exist, and common names can get confusing. Virtually all of the mints can be grown in the Southwest, if you pamper them and give them ample moisture. Indeed, they can get invasive if given too much moisture, so ideally grow them in pots raised off the soil, so they can't escape out the bottom. If you grow them in a water garden, in pots with the bottom inch underwater, you do not need to worry if you forget to water one single summer day. Note that in the Cool Highland and Cold Mountain gardens, you will need to protect your pots of mint in the winter; the moist soil may freeze and crack the pots.

■ Recommended Varieties

There are many different varieties of mint. Experi*mint*!

■ When and Where to Plant

Temperature: Mints are semi-evergreen and may appear to be dead during the cold winter months. Not to worry, they will reappear in spring. Mint will become established best if planted after danger of frost has passed.

Soil: Mint is widely adaptable to most soils but does best with pH of 6.2 to 7.2, thus amended garden soil is recommended.

Sun: Full sun to partial shade.

■ How to Plant

Starting seeds indoors: Grow mint from cuttings. If you know someone who has mint, just cut a few stems and stick them in water to root.

Planting outside: Once the cuttings have rooted, plant them outside in a large pot. Do not plant them in the ground, they will invade other areas of your garden.

■ How to Grow

Water: Mint requires ample moisture, making it an ideal plant for a water garden in the Desert zones. Place pot with bottom inch under water.

Fertilizer: No extra fertilizer is needed.

Pest control: Mint has no major pest problems.

■ When and How to Harvest

The tender new leaves are the most flavorful without being bitter. Cut the tips off periodically even if you don't have immediate need, this encourages ample new growth. Don't throw out the trimmings! Dry trimmings for mint tea or culinary use, especially popular in Indian cuisine.

Children will appreciate the many different varieties of mint, like this chocolate mint.

OREGANO & MARJORAM
(*Origanum vulgare*) and (*Origanum majorana*)

Oregano is often known as the "pizza" herb.

Oregano, Greek oregano, Roman oregano, and marjoram are all simply different cultivars of the same species, although sometimes divided into subspecies or variety depending on degree of "hairyness." These perennial herbs are native to the hills of Greece, which means they can take some of our heat, but not 100 degrees for 100 days. It can also take some cold, but not much below 20°F for very long. If you live in a Desert zone, they will be perennial plants, lasting many years. When selecting plants for your Desert garden, first select where you plan on planting them. The hotter the location, the more hairy plants will survive better. I bought one of each type and planted the Greek and Roman oregano in full sun and the plain oregano and marjoram where they got afternoon shade in summer. All have thrived, and produce prolifically.

■ Recommended Varieties
There are well over 100 cultivars of oregano, some advertised to have a hint of "cinnamon." Try different ones to get just the right one for your palate.

■ When and Where to Plant
Temperature: Plant oregano and marjoram outside after danger of frost has passed.
Soil: Oregano grows best in well-drained soil with a pH of 6.5 to 7.5.
Sun: Full sun to part shade for marjoram, especially in the Desert zones.

■ How to Plant
Starting seeds indoors: You can start seeds indoors or sow directly outside. It is easier to grow from transplants from the nursery.

Growing oregano in a pot ensures it won't hog all of the space in your vegetable garden.

Planting outside: Space plants 8 inches apart. In Desert gardens they can be planted as part of the landscape. In upper elevations, treat them as annuals, or plant in containers and bring them indoors in winter.

How to Grow

Water: Water is needed on a fairly regular basis, especially in a Southwestern summer.

Fertilizer: I never bother to fertilize my oregano or marjoram because I have so much of it. You can fertilize with a general purpose fertilizer in any nonfreezing month.

Pest control: Few pests bother oregano unless it is drought. If you see signs of insect damage, make sure you are watering it enough—or allowing it to dry somewhat if too wet.

When and How to Harvest

Leaves are most fragrant just before the flowers open, but you can snip leaves off to use at any time. Snip off the tender new growth for use in fresh salads. Snip woody growth and strip the leaves for cooking. Oregano and marjoram dry well and can be stored for a year or so before losing flavor. You can make gift sets of homegrown Southwestern landscape herbs including oregano, marjoram, rosemary, and thyme for folks "Back East."

ROSEMARY & GERMANDER

(*Rosmarinus officinalis*) and (*Teucrium chamaedrys*)

Rosemary and creeping germander are woody, evergreen perennial herbs native to the Mediterranean. Both of these plants are culinary herbs grown as landscape plants throughout the warmer areas of the Southwest. Both thrive in well-drained soil that is on the alkaline side. They are easy to grow once established and fun to cook with. You can use fresh rosemary or germander when roasting meats and vegetables. Rosemary twigs make excellent kebab sticks for grilling. Plan on planting both of these tasty herbs. Rosemary and germander are cold hardy in the Desert zones but will need to be grown as an annual or in containers in the cooler zones. You can bring them indoors in the winter, but they do better in the moving air outdoors in any nonfreezing month.

■ *Recommended Varieties*

There are many varieties to try. Do you want creeping forms for the landscape or do you prefer the upright forms?

ROSEMARY: Leaves are needle-like and bluish green. 'Shish Kabob' rosemary has an upright growth form with long, straight stems that are great for shish kabobs for grilling. 'Bennington Blue' has dark blue flowers. 'Mrs. Howard's Creeping' rosemary has light blue flowers. 'Arp' and 'Blue Spires' are two of the most cold-hardy rosemaries, and may survive in a sheltered location in the Cool Highland Zone.

GERMANDER: With dark green waxy leaves, germander looks beautiful in the landscape. There are not many varieties available beyond creeping or upright. Note that there are other species, but they are not generally for culinary use.

■ *When and Where to Plant*

Temperature: Plant transplants outside after danger of frost has passed for best establishment.

Soil: Rosemary and germander are widely adaptable to many different soil types but both need well-drained soil, and do best in pH 6.2 to 7.2.

Sun: Full sun to afternoon shade in the Low Desert.

How to Plant

Starting seeds indoors: Not recommended.

Planting outside: It is much easier to grow rosemary and germander from transplants than to attempt to grow them from seed. Plant transplants outside where they'll have room to grow to be 2 to 3 feet wide and up to 3 feet tall (depending on variety).

When and How to Grow

Water: Pampered plants from the nursery are used to getting water every single day. Slowly wean them off this regime. Once plants are established, water to 2 feet deep at least once a month in summer, more often in sandy soils.

Fertilizer: No extra fertilizer is needed, but I like to provide a bloom fertilizer in spring to encourage flowering and entice pollinators into the garden.

Use thick, straight branches of rosemary as shish kabob sticks.

Pest control: Stressed plants may get mealybugs or scale. Use horticultural oil to treat the plants once you see pests and avoid using as an herb for two months afterwards. Outdoors, drought stress may affect the plants. Indoors, stress may be due to lack of light or excessive watering. If you grow these herbs indoors, give them a summer vacation on a shady porch to help eliminate pests.

When and How to Harvest

Cut pieces of rosemary or germander at any time of the year to use for cooking. The young tips can be tasty mixed into fresh salads. The rest of the plant is good for use in soups, stews, or roasting. You can also dry the leaves when you trim the plant to size. (If you have an abundance of dried leaves, send them "Back East" as a holiday gift!) Use the dried material within eighteen months before the flavorful oils degrade.

SWEET MARIGOLD
(Tagetes lucida)

Sweet marigold is a good substitute for tarragon.

This plant has more common names than you can shake a stick at, a clear indication of how useful it is considered in all the places it grows. It is variously called winter tarragon, Texas tarragon, false tarragon, Mexican tarragon, Spanish tarragon, and even Florida tarragon, as well as Mexican mint marigold, sweet-scented marigold, Mt. Pima marigold, pericon, yerba anis, and Iya. As you may have guessed, the leaves have a tarragon-like flavor. Many chefs are now using sweet marigold as a substitute for French tarragon, especially in winter when the real thing is hard to get, and in hot climates where French tarragon just won't grow. Sweet marigold is, however, a little stronger than tarragon and has more of an anise flavor. Leaves can be used anywhere you would use tarragon, and indeed, in additional ways since the refreshing flavor blends well with sweet creations, like chocolate dishes.

Sweet marigold is a perennial in the Desert zones, and annual if planted in the ground in the Upper zones. If heavily mulched for winter it may survive in the Cool Highlands. It can also be planted in pots and brought indoors in winter.

Sweet marigold is often used as a medicinal plant because all parts of the plant are high in antibacterial compounds. Since even the roots of these marigolds kill bacteria, you should never plant any marigolds next to members of the pea or bean family, which rely on root bacteria for their nutrition.

■ Recommended Cultivars & Varieties

In Mexico and Guatemala, almost every upland village has its own unnamed cultivar of sweet marigold. Some folks swear by the oval leaf form while others are just as adamant that the narrow leaves are better. Having grown well over thirty of these, I advocate getting any plant you can, and find the spot in your garden where it thrives for you. You may lose a few but keep trying, the flavor is worth it. Seed-grown often do better than cuttings.

■ *When and Where to Plant*

In Low Desert this mountain herb will need to be grown in terra cotta pots in the shade or in the water garden. In Middle Desert, plant so that it gets afternoon shade in summer. In Upper elevations, plant in full sun.

Temperature: This herb grows better in cooler soils, but needs at least 65°F soils to germinate.

Soil: Found in the wild in soils of a wide pH range, 6.5 to 8.0, including limestone and serpentine soils. Does best in well-drained soils.

Sun: Depending on season and elevation, full sun to full shade.

■ *How to Plant*

Starting seeds indoors: You can start seed indoors at any time, at least six weeks before transplanting outdoors.

Planting outside: After last frost, sow seed ¼ inch deep and two to three seeds per inch. Keep evenly moist until germination and thin the seedlings to 4 to 6 inches apart. Use these thinnings for salad, etc. They have that lovely tarragonish flavor.

■ *How to Grow*

Water: Some drying tolerated, but prefers watering at least once per week in summer.

Fertilizer: If you wish to use as a culinary herb, sidedress with a high-nitrogen fertilizer once per month in any nonfrost month. Once bloom begins, you can add a bloom fertilizer, for ample blooms will encourage pollinators to visit your garden.

Pest control: No pests appear to bother this plant.

■ *When and How to Harvest*

Use fresh flowers and leaves of sweet marigold in salads or in cooking and baking. As with any aromatic herb, add to soups, sauces, chicken dishes, etc., near the end of cooking so the flavors will not be lost in cooking. Sweet marigold imparts delightful flavor to remoulade, tartar and béarnaise sauces, French salad dressing, and bouquet garni. Use chopped leaves to make herb butter or cheese spread, and don't forget to use in fish and egg dishes (especially in a French-style omelet). Ideally, use this herb fresh in cooking because some flavor is lost in drying. To preserve, it is better to freeze the leaves or infuse them into vinegar. Harvest by snipping off the last few inches from new fast-growing tips. The flowers look lovely in a bottle of herbal vinegar, plus they do impart flavor. One additional way everyone can enjoy sweet marigold is in fresh flower arrangements. Branches perfume and brighten floral arrangements, and appear to help keep water-borne wilt bacteria at bay.

THYME *(Thymus* spp.)

Thyme is a large and very popular genus, with over 350 species and countless cultivars grown around the world. Aside from looking lovely in the landscape, thyme is a strong herb used in cooking, and has some proven medicinal properties as well. Thyme can also be used in potpourri, herb pillows, and in herbal soaps and lotions. Its refreshing scent tops any artificial room freshener on the market.

The center of origin and center of diversity for this lovely, fragrant, tasty, and healthful herb is the rocky slopes of the mountains of the eastern Mediterranean region, in the area that is now mostly Greece. Since they are pre-adapted to low water conditions, most species of thyme can be grown here. I grow my thyme plants where they get roof run-off, thus I rarely need to water them; and yet they offer a lush look to my entryway with their glossy green leaves.

Thyme is indispensable for cooking savory dishes. Use it in everything from roast chicken to vegetable soup to shortbread cookies. If you're interested in making your own flavored vinegars, thyme is a good herb to try. Thyme can be cut back or replanted every few years for fresh new growth. There are more than a hundred varieties of thyme, including some sharply flavored ones that are hardy in the Cold Mountains.

■ *Recommended Varieties*

There are many thymes to choose from, but here are the species most commonly found in the nursery.

COMMON OR CULINARY THYME (*Thymus vulgaris*): Is a low woody plant barely reaching a foot tall. It quickly becomes leggy with bare wood showing so harvest and use or dry your thyme often.

CREEPING THYME (*Thymus praecox*): Makes an attractive and useful groundcover. It is culinary, too! Harvest as needed.

LEMON THYME (*Thymus* x *citriodorus*): Is a delicious and fragrant low-growing variety with glossy green leaves, and goes wonderfully with fish dishes.

GOLDEN LEMON THYME (*Thymus* x *citriodorus* 'Aureus'): Equally fragrant and delicious. With wonderfully variegated leaves, it looks good in the landscape.

MOTHER-OF-THYME (*Thymus serpyllum*) AND WOOLLY THYME (*Thymus pseudolanuginosis*): Not generally used as culinary herbs, these two popular species of creeping thyme are useful in the landscape. Both grow well between shady flagstones, and can be used to help stabilize shady banks that get enough water.

■ When and Where to Plant

Temperature: Thyme grows best in warm temperatures. Plant thyme plants outside after all danger of frost has passed for best results.

Soil: Thyme needs well-drained soil to grow. It will quickly rot if kept consistently wet. Ideally, pH should be 6.2 to 7.2.

Sun: Full sun to full shade in Low and Middle Desert Zones.

■ How to Plant

Starting seeds indoors: Not recommended. It is easier to grow from cuttings or nursery seedlings.

Planting outside: It is much easier to grow thyme from cuttings than it is to grow it from seed. Root cuttings by snipping off 4-inch pieces of fresh, green growth from a plant. Strip the leaves off the lower half and place in water. Once the plant has developed roots, transplant it outside.

■ How to Grow

Water: Once established, thyme still has a shallow root system and will need water, generally at least once a week in summer.

Fertilizer: Fertilize once a year in spring with a balanced fertilizer.

Pest control: Aphids and spider mites will attack the plant if it is stressed. You may need to add extra water.

■ When and How to Harvest

Thyme leaves are most fragrant if they are cut before the plant flowers. Keep cutting back the top 4 to 6 inches of growth to stimulate fresh, new growth, which is best for cooking. Sprinkle thyme fresh or dried in soups, salads, on meat dishes or in herb breads. Use an ample number of sprigs in herbal vinegars and oils for an intense and refreshing flavor. Thyme is used in a dish popular in the region of Catalonia in northeastern Spain. Called *Sopa de Farigola*, or Thyme Soup, fresh eggs and day-old bread are topped with boiling broth made from water, sprigs of thyme, and some olive oil.

Thyme is found in the herb blend *za'atar*. Confusingly, *za'atar* is a general name for any Middle Eastern herb from four different genera *Origanum* (oregano), *Calamintha* (calamint), *Thymus* (thyme), and *Satureja* (savory). The blend *za'atar* is made from any combination of two or more of the above herbs, dried and mixed together with sesame seeds, dried sumac, often salt, and a variety of other spices.

Harvest thyme before the flowers appear.

RESOURCES

While not comprehensive (it would take pages), this list offers some fairly local resources to get you started growing your own vegetables and fruits. I have grown and tested products from virtually every resource listed here and can say that (at least some of) their products will do well in our unique region. Many of these companies have websites that offer valuable growing tips.

Arbico Organics
(Integrated Pest Management
  supplies)
P.O. Box 8910
Tucson, AZ 85738
800-827-2847
www.arbico-organics.com

Baker Creek Heirloom Seeds
(Vegetable seeds)
2278 Baker Creek Road
Mansfield, MO 65704
417-924-8917
www.rareseeds.com

Botanical Interests
(Vegetable and herb seeds)
660 Compton Street
Broomfield, CO 80020
877-821-4340
www.botanicalinterests.com

Bountiful Gardens
(Vegetable and herb seeds,
  fruit tree and shrub seeds)
1712-D S. Main Street
Willits, CA 95490-4400
707-459-6410
www.bountifulgardens.org

Burnt Ridge Nursery & Orchards
432 Burnt Ridge Road
Onalaska, WA 98570
360-985-2873
www.burntridgenursery.com

Dixondale Farms
(Onions)
P. O. Box 129
Carrizo Springs, TX 78834
877-367-1015
www.dixondalefarms.com

Forest Farm
(Fruit trees and shrubs, herbs)
990 Tetherow Road
Williams, OR 97544
541-846-7269
www.forestfarm.com

High Country Gardens
(Fruit trees and shrubs, herbs)
2902 Rufina Street
Santa Fe, NM 87507
800-925-9387
www.highcountrygardens.com

Gardens Alive
(IPM, soil inoculants)
5100 Schenley Place
Lawrenceburg, Indiana 47025
513-354-1482
www.gardensalive.com

High Mowing Organic Seeds
(Organic vegetable seeds)
76 Quarry Road
Wolcott, VT 05680
802-472-6174
www.highmowingseeds.com

Kitazawa Seed Co.
(Asian vegetable seeds and herbs)
201 4th Street, Unit 206
Oakland, CA 94607
510-595-1188
www.kitazawaseed.com

Native Seeds/SEARCH
(Vegetable and herb seed)
3584 E. River Road
Tucson, AZ 85718
520-622-0830
www.nativeseeds.org

One Green World
(Fruit trees)
6469 S.E. 134th Ave.
Portland, OR 97236-4540
877-353-4028
www.onegreenworld.com

Peaceful Valley Supply
(Vegetable seed, IPM, fruit nursery)
P. O. Box 2209
Grass Valley, CA 95945
888-784-1722
www.groworganic.com
Retail outlet in Grass Valley

Plants of the Southwest
(Seeds, herbs, fruits, and nursery)
3095 Aqua Fria
Santa Fe, NM 87507
505-471-2212
www.plantsofthesouthwest.com
retail outlets in Santa Fe
    and Albuquerque

Renee's Garden Seed
(Vegetable and herb seed,
    including organic)
6060 Graham Hill Road
Felton, CA 95018
888-880-7228
www.reneesgarden.com

Raintree Nursery
(Fruit trees and shrubs)
391 Butts Road
Morton, WA 98356
800-391-8892
www.raintreenursery.com

Seed Savers Exchange
(Vegetable and herb seed)
3094 N. Winn Road
Decorah, IA 52101
563-382-5990
www.seedsavers.org

Seeds of Change
(Organic vegetable and herb seed)
c/o Marketing Concepts
P. O. Box 152
Spicer, MN 56288
888-762-7333
www.seedsofchange.com

Southern Exposure Seed Exchange
(Vegetable and herb seeds)
P. O. Box 460
Mineral, VA 23117
540-894-9480
www.SouthernExposure.com

Terrior Seeds
(Heirloom vegetable and herb seed)
P. O. Box 4995
Chino Valley, AZ 86323
888-878-5247
www.UnderwoodGardens.com

Tomato Growers Supply Co.
(Vegetable seeds)
P. O. Box 60015
Ft. Myers, FL 33906
888-768-3476
www.tomatogrowers.com

Local Botanical Gardens, Arboreta, and Zoological Parks

Often overlooked when it comes to gardening for food, don't forget these nearby places that grow plants. They often have a wealth of knowledge to share, including mature examples of any number of the fruits and herbs mentioned in this book. Many public gardens also showcase vegetable gardens, and demonstrations of composting. Weekend workshops abound! Don't forget zoological parks, most of them have one or more trained horticulturists on staff.

Cooperative Extension Service

Your local County Cooperative Extension Service is an invaluable resource, but you may not think so when you try to use their websites—which can be clumsy to navigate. When possible, give the office in your county a call and ask the volunteer Master Gardeners your question(s). While enthusiastic about gardening, some of these Master Gardeners are new to the Southwest, thus you may benefit by calling with the same question on another day.

Arizona (search by your county for most useful information)
http://extension.arizona.edu

Colorado (useful for Cool Highlands and Cold Mountain zones)
www.ext.colostate.edu/index.html

Nevada (search both "Agriculture" and "Horticulture" publications)
www.unce.unr.edu

New Mexico (search by your county for most useful information)
http://extension.nmsu.edu

GLOSSARY

Acidic soil: The pH scale ranges from 0 to 14, with 7.0 being neutral. Acidic soil has a pH lower than 7.0. Most garden plants prefer soil a bit on the acidic side.

Afternoon sun: A garden with full sun from 1:00 to 5:00 p.m. daily, with shade during the morning hours.

Alkaline soil: On a soil pH scale of 0 to 14, alkaline soil has a pH higher than 7.0. Southwestern soils are typically alkaline.

Annual: A plant that germinates (sprouts), grows to maturity, flowers, and dies within one season or year.

***Bacillus thuringiensis* or Bt**: A species of naturally occurring soil bacteria that is toxic to all members of the butterfly family. It can be legally used as an organic pest control agent and is often cloned into bioengineered (GMO) plants.

Bare root: Soil is removed from the roots of dormant plants and they are shipped and sold. Fruit trees and roses are often sold bare root, but this often leads to plant failure in the arid Southwest.

Beneficial insects: These insects perform valuable services such as pollination and pest control. Ladybugs, preying mantises, and bees are some examples.

Biennial: A plant that grows during the first year, goes dormant, then resprouts, flowers and dies in the second year. Many root vegetables are technically biennials.

Bolting: Annual and biennial plants grow and store energy until the time to flower nears, then they switch from storing energy to producing flowers and seeds, after which they die. If it is a crop you wish to eat, like lettuce or herbs, bolting is undesirable as the foliage becomes bitter. Bolting appears to occur quite suddenly but if you note days to maturity on your seed packet, you will discover it is a highly predictable event.

Brown materials: One part of a well-balanced compost bin, brown materials include high-carbon materials such as dried leaves, plant stems, dryer lint, and even shredded newspaper.

Bud: The bud is an undeveloped shoot nestled between the leaf and the stem that will eventually produce another leaf, a flower, or a branch.

Bush: Shrubs are often referred to as bushes.

Caliche: Caliche is a type of sedimentary rock formed from calcium carbonate and prevalent in Southwestern soils. Discussed more fully in Chapter 3.

Compost: Organic matter that has been decomposed and recycled so it can be used as a fertilizer and soil amendment.

Canopy: The outermost foliage of a tree or shrub.

Central leader: The term for the center trunk of a tree or shrub.

Chilling hours: Hours when the air temperature is below 45°F; chilling hours are related to fruit production.

Common name: A name that is generally used to identify a plant and can vary from region to region, as opposed to a botanical name, which is standard throughout the world. Unshiu, satsuma tangerine, and cold hardy mandarin all refer to a single plant, *Citrus unshiu*.

Contact herbicide: This type of herbicide kills only the part of the plant that it touches.

Container: Any vessel that is used for planting; containers can be of ceramic, clay, steel, plastic, or even old Army boots.

Container grown: This describes a plant that is grown, sold, and shipped while in a pot.

Cool-season annual: This is a flowering plant, such as snapdragon or pansy, that thrives during cooler months.

Cool-season vegetable: This is a vegetable, such as spinach, broccoli, or peas, that thrives during cooler months.

Cover crop: Plants grown specifically to cover the soil during nongrowing season, and are often selected for their ability to enrich the soil, prevent erosion, suppress weeds, and control pests and diseases.

Cross-pollinate: This describes the transfer of pollen from one plant to another plant of the same species and genetic line (not the same forming a hybrid).

Dappled shade: This is bright shade created by high tree branches or tree foliage, where patches of sunlight and shade intermingle.

Day-neutral plant: A plant that flowers when it reaches a certain size, regardless of the day length, is a day-neutral plant.

Deadhead: Remove dead flowers in order to encourage further bloom and prevent the plant from going to seed.

Deciduous: A plant that loses all its leaves and is bare for a season, typically in winter.

Diatomaceous earth: Used as a natural control for ants, flea beetles, and other garden pests, diatomaceous earth is composed of the remains of microscopic diatoms, a type of sea creature.

Dormancy: The period when plants stop growing for a season to conserve either moisture or energy, this naturally occurs according to genetic programming.

Drip line: The line around the outermost edge of the canopy of a tree or shrub where a light rain drips off to hit the soil. This is the area where most of the roots that absorb water and nutrients are found. (Anchoring roots are near the trunk.)

Drip irrigation: A system of watering that allows water to drip out of drip emitters at a slow rate, allowing the water to soak into the soil and reducing the amount of irrigation water lost to evaporation.

Dwarf: In fruit gardening, a dwarf tree grows no taller than 10 feet tall. Commonly normal fruit scions are grafted onto dwarfing rootstocks.

Evergreen: A plant that remains covered in foliage year-round. Ironically, evergreens may grow new leaves and shed the old all at once, so you may still have to rake leaves seasonally.

Floating row covers: Lightweight fabric that allows sunlight to reach plants, the cover is generally placed on hoops and used to protect plants from pests. Usually white in color.

Flower stalk: The stem that supports the flower and elevates it above the foliage for pollination.

Frost: Ice crystals that form when the temperature falls below freezing (32°F) create frost.

Full sun: Areas of the garden that receive direct sunlight for six to eight hours a day or more.

Fungicide: This describes a chemical compound used to control fungal diseases.

Garden soil: The existing soil in a garden bed; it is generally evaluated by its nutrient content and texture. Garden soil is also sold as a bagged item at nurseries and garden centers.

Germination: The process in which a plant emerges from a seed.

GMO (genetically modified organism): refers to seed whose genetic material has been altered using genetic engineering techniques, inserting genes from an entirely different life form such as bacteria.

Grafted tree: This is a tree composed of two parts: the top, or scion, which bears fruit, and the bottom, or rootstock.

Graft union: This is the place on a fruit tree trunk where the rootstock and the scion have been joined.

Granular fertilizer: This type of fertilizer comes in a dry, pellet-like form rather than a liquid or powder.

Green materials: One part of a well-balanced compost bin, green materials include kitchen scraps, garden thinnings, and manure, adding valuable nitrogen to the compost.

Gypsum: Gypsum is calcium sulfate and can be useful in Southwest soils when used according to label instructions, but can add to your problems if not used correctly.

Hardening off: This is the process of slowly acclimating seedlings and young plants grown in an indoor environment to the outdoors.

Hardiness zone map: This map lists average annual minimum temperature ranges of a particular area. North America is divided into eleven separate cold-hardiness zones, but these are not exactly useful to predict plant ability to withstand a Southwestern summer.

Heirloom: refers to plant varieties that were popular half a century or more ago, chiefly prior to World War II. Heirloom varieties are generally open-pollinated as well, but the terms are not interchangeable. There are a number of heirlooms from the 1500s available for our Southwestern gardens.

Hybrid: Plants produced by crossing plants from two genetically distinct lines, hybrids are chosen to desirable characteristics such as disease resistance. Hybrids are commonly sterile (unable to produce seed).

Insecticide: A substance is used for destroying or controlling insects. Insecticides are available in organic and synthetic formulations, but kill all insects, even beneficial ones.

Integrated Pest Management (IPM): IPM includes managing insects, plant pathogens, and weeds and emphasizes the growth of a healthy crop with the least possible disruption to an ecosystem by encouraging natural pest control mechanisms such as ladybugs.

Irrigation: A system of watering the landscape, irrigation can be an in-ground automatic system, soaker or drip hoses, or hand-held hoses with nozzles.

Larva: The immature stage of an insect that goes through complete metamorphosis; a caterpillar is the larva of a butterfly or moth. The plural is larvae.

Lime: Lime is calcium carbonate, a soil additive used to correct calcium deficiencies and raise pH in acidic soils. Avoid using this product on alkaline soils.

Liquid fertilizer: Plant fertilizer in a liquid form; some types need to be mixed with water, and some types are ready to use from the bottle.

Long-day plant: Plants that flower when the days are longer than their critical photoperiod. Long-day plants typically flower in early summer, when the days are still getting longer.

Morning sun: Areas of the garden that have an eastern exposure and receive direct sun in the morning hours.

Mulch: Any type of material that is spread over the soil surface around the base of plants to suppress weeds and retain soil moisture.

Nematode: Microscopic, worm-like organisms that live in the soil; some nematodes are beneficial, while others are harmful.

New wood (new growth): The new growth on plants, it is characterized by a greener, more tender form than older, woodier growth.

Old wood: Old wood is growth that is more than one year old. Some fruit plants produce on old wood. If you prune these plants in spring before they flower and fruit, you will cut off the wood that will produce fruit.

Open pollinated: This is used for a plant that produces stable characteristics from generation to generation when grown in a garden setting. In other words, it often self-pollinates itself.

Organic: This term describes products derived from naturally occurring materials instead of synthesized materials.

Part shade: Areas of the garden that receive more sun than shade in a single day. Term applies to plants that need protection from mid-day sun.

Part sun: Areas of the garden that receive some sun but more shade each day. The term should not be used interchangeably with "part shade," because a "part sun" designation places greater emphasis on the minimal sun requirements.

Perennial: A plant that lives for more than two years is a perennial. It is generally applied to nonwoody plants like iris.

pH: A value designating the acidity or the alkalinity of garden soil, pH is measured on a scale of 1 to 14, with 7.0 being neutral.

Pinch: A method of removing unwanted plant growth, promoting bushier growth and increased blooming. Although it implies using your fingers, you can pinch (basil for example) with scissors or prunners.

Pollination: Needed before a plant will produce fruit, pollination refers to the transfer of pollen from the male pollen-bearing structure (stamen) to the receptive female structure (pistil). Pollination can be done by wind, bees, butterflies, moths, or hummingbirds.

Powdery mildew: A fungal disease characterized by white powdery spots on plant leaves and stems.

Pre-emergent herbicide: Applied to the soil, this chemical blocks all seeds from ever sprouting. It can persist in soils for years.

Pruning: This is a garden task in which a variety of tools are used to remove dead or overgrown branches to increase plant fullness and health.

Rootball: The network of roots and soil clinging to a plant when it is lifted out of the growing container or ground.

Rootstock: The bottom part of a grafted plant, rootstocks are often used to create dwarf fruit trees, impart pest or disease resistance, or make a plant more cold hardy.

Scientific name: A two-word identification system that consists of the genus and species of a plant, and is universal around the globe such as *Prunus amygdalus* for the almond.

Scion: The top part of a grafted plant, in the case of fruit trees, this is the part that bears fruit.

Seed-starting mix: Typically a soilless blend of perlite, vermiculite, peat moss, and other ingredients, seed-starting mix is specifically formulated for growing plants from seed.

Self-fertile: A plant that can cross with itself and does not require cross-pollination from another plant in order to produce fruit and seed.

Semi-dwarf: A fruit tree grafted onto a rootstock that restricts growth of the tree to one-half to two-thirds of its natural size.

Shade: Garden shade is the absence of any direct sunlight in a given area, usually due to tree foliage or building shadows.

Shade cloth: Used to reduce the amount of sunlight that reaches plants, shade cloth is rated by the percent shade it provides. Shade cloth can help protect tender transplants or extend the season of cool-season crops as the weather warms.

Short-day plant: Flowering when the length of day is shorter than its critical photoperiod, short-day plants typically bloom during fall, winter, or early spring.

Shrub: This is a nontechnical designation for a woody plant generally with multiple trunks and a height generally less than 10 feet. Many fruit "trees" are very shrubby in nature.

Sidedress: To sprinkle slow-release fertilizer along the side of a plant row.

Slow-release fertilizer: Fertilizer encapsulated so that it releases nutrients at a slower rate throughout the season, requiring less-frequent applications. Often clay is used in making these fertilizers and thus they are not ideal for Southwestern soils.

Soaker hose: A porous hose, made from plastic rubber or cloth that allows water to seep out all along the length of the hose. These are handy in the garden by subject to decay by sunlight.

Soil test: An analysis of a soil sample, this determines the level of nutrients (to identify deficiencies) and detects pH.

Standard: Describing a fruit tree grown on its own seedling rootstock or a non-dwarfing rootstock, this is the largest of the three sizes of fruit trees.

Sucker: The growth from the base of a tree or a woody plant, often caused by stress, they often occur below the graft of a fruit tree and should be removed. Suckers commonly occur after a frost or excessive UV exposure.

Sulfur: An essential mineral used as a soil additive, sulfur acts to chemically unbind the soil minerals (nutrients) so that plants can use them.

Systemic: This type of chemical is absorbed by the roots of a plant and spreads through the plant's entire system. There are both systemic pesticides and systemic herbicides.

Taproot: The enlarged, tapered plant root that grows vertically downward, a carrot is one tasty taproot.

Temperate plant: Plant whose ancestors are from temperate regions of the world where cold winters are the norm, and thus genetically programmed for either life in a single season or an ability to overwinter. Cabbage and carrots are temperate climate plants.

Thinning: (1) The practice of removing excess plants in a row of vegetables to leave more room for the remaining vegetables to grow. (2) Removing a number of fruits from fruit trees when the fruits are still small so that the remaining fruits can grow larger. (3) Removing a certain amount of foliage from a perennial plant canopy to encourage light and air to enter the center of the plant.

Topdress: Fertilizer spread on top of the soil around the base of (usually) fruit trees.

Transplants: Plants grown in one location, then replanted in another; seeds started indoors or nursery plants are transplanted into the garden.

Tree: A woody perennial plant typically over 10 feet tall and generally with a single trunk.

Tropical plant: Plant whose ancestors are from tropical regions of the world, and thus genetically programmed for a warm climate. Tropicals like citrus and basil are not hardy to frost.

Warm-season vegetable: This is a vegetable that thrives during the warmer months. Examples are tomatoes, okra, and peppers. These vegetables do not tolerate frost.

INDEX

PHOTO CREDITS

Curtis Clark/cc-by-2.5: pp. 60

Tom Eltzroth: pp. 181, 193

Katie Elzer-Peters: pp. 19, 20, 23, 26 (both), 33, 37, 38, 42, 44 (top and middle), 45 (all), 46 (lower 3), 47 (all), 48 (all), 49 (right), 50, 51 (both), 53, 54, 58, 112, 113, 114, 116, 123, 126, 130, 135, 138, 142, 145 (lower), 146, 148, 150, 155, 163, 172, 174, 175, 176, 179, 190, 196, 205

iStock: pp. 21, 84, 101, 140, 143, 173, 182, 199, 202

Jerry Pavia: pp. 90

Shutterstock: pp. 6, 10, 11, 31, 35, 39, 43, 46 (top 2), 49 (left), 57, 61, 62, 64, 66, 69, 76, 78, 81, 82, 87, 88, 92, 94, 96, 98, 104, 107, 110, 118, 124, 129, 132, 136, 149, 151, 152, 157, 158, 161, 164, 167, 168, 185, 186, 187, 189, 197, 201

6th Happiness/cc-by-3.0: pp. 52

Forest & Kim Starr/cc-by-3.0: pp. 72

Lynn Steiner: pp. 145 (top), 198

David R. Tribble/cc-by-3.0: pp. 28

Wikimedia Commons/cc-by-3.0: pp. 194

MEET JACQUELINE A. SOULE

Jacqueline Soule is a longtime Southwestern gardener and award-winning garden writer, her first gardening article appearing in 1983. Of her ten published books, eight are on gardening in our unique climate. She has been a popular columnist for many years with weekly and monthly *Gardening With Soule* and other regular columns in a number of national, regional and local publications, including *Arizona/Nevada Lovin' Life* newspaper, *Explorer* newspaper and *Angie's List* magazine.

Jacqueline grew up in Tucson, and obtained a B.S. in horticulture and a B.S. in ecology, evolutionary biology from the University of Arizona both with honors and *cum laude*, then left Tucson to experience life "Back East." Academically she acquired an M.S. in botany from Michigan State University, and a Ph.D. in botany from the University of Texas, while she discovered gardening in various climates. Included in Dr. Soule's "Back East" sojourns were positions in botanical gardens and arboreta including the Morris Arboretum in Philadelphia, Chicago Botanic Garden, and the Frederik Meijer Gardens and Sculpture Park in Grand Rapids.

Jacqueline joyously returned to the Southwest in 1997, and has been active in the plant and gardening community ever since, serving in various offices in plant societies, clubs, and organizations both locally and beyond, including the board of the international Desert Legume Program. She hosted the Garden Writers Association National Symposium in Tucson in 2012. Along with Horticultural Therapy programs through the Tucson Botanical Gardens, Jacqueline offers numerous lectures, presentations and community classes on plants and gardening for all ages and in various venues around the region, all while earning a living as a garden writer.

Jacqueline's garden is the entire landscape around her home, filled with herbs, fruiting plants, raised beds, and containers. There is something to harvest virtually every day of the year from the garden or yard. Thus, Jacqueline prefers plants that need as little care as possible, because there is just so much! Her husband, Paul, appreciates this, since he often gets called on to water and help weed. Virtually every plant, garden implement, and soil amendment in this book has been tested or grown in Jacqueline's garden at one time or another.